齊物
逍遙
2 0 2 4 II

黃效文——著

ENLIGHTENED SOJOURN

Authored and Photographed by Wong How Man

Wong How Man

Time Magazine honored Wong How Man among their 25 Asian Heroes in 2002, calling Wong "China's most accomplished living explorer". CNN has featured his work over a dozen times, including a half-hour profile by the network's anchor. Discovery Channel has made several documentaries about his work. The Wall Street Journal has also featured him on its front page. Wong began exploring China in 1974. He is Founder/President of the China Exploration & Research Society, a non-profit organization founded in 1986 specializing in exploration, research, conservation and education in remote China and neighboring countries. Wong has led six major expeditions for the National Geographic. He successfully defined the sources of the Yangtze, Mekong, Yellow River, Salween, Irrawaddy and the Brahmaputra rivers.

He conducts projects in Mainland China, India, Nepal, Bhutan, Laos, Myanmar, the Philippines, and also Taiwan. In these countries or regions, he has set up centers, theme exhibits, or permanent operation bases. Wong has authored over thirty books and has received many accolades, among them an honorary doctorate from his alma mater, the University of Wisconsin at River Falls, and the Lifetime Achievement Award from Monk Hsing Yun of Taiwan. He has been invited as keynote speaker at many international functions.

In 2023, the University of Hong Kong established the Wong How Man Centre for Exploration in order to perpetuate the legacy of his work into the future.

黃
效
文

《時代雜誌》在二〇〇二年曾選黃效文為亞洲二十五位英雄之一，稱他為「中國最有成就的在世探險家」。CNN 報導過黃效文的各項工作超過十二次之多，其中還包括主播 Richard Quest 的三十分鐘專訪。探索頻道也為他做的工作製作了好幾個紀錄片。《華爾街日報》也曾用頭版報導過他。

黃效文自一九七四年開始在中國探險。他是中國探險學會的創辦人和會長，這是個非營利組織，致力於在中國偏遠地區及鄰近國家的探險、研究、保育和教育工作。他曾經在美國《國家地理雜誌》帶領過六個重要的探險。他成功地定位的源頭包括長江、湄公河、黃河、薩爾溫江、伊洛瓦底江及雅魯藏布江。

他的學會主導的文化和自然保育項目橫跨中國和鄰近的國家，包括印度、尼泊爾、不丹、寮國、緬甸、菲律賓還有台灣。黃效文著作的書超過三十本並獲得過許多榮譽，他的母校威斯康辛大學頒發給他名譽博士學位，星雲大師也贈與他「華人世界終身成就獎」。他也是許多國際會議裡的專題演講人。

二〇二三年，香港大學成立了黃效文探險中心，以傳承他畢生的事業，並力圖讓他的精神與貢獻在未來繼續閃耀。

Foreword by George Yeo
Former Foreign Minister of Singapore

Enlightened Sojourn is a delicious collection of some of How Man's field reports over the last 50 years. He is a wonderful story teller. Through his accounts, we are invited to share his experiences of people and places. These are experiences we wish for ourselves but often can't have because they are off the beaten track and with individuals we only read about. His choice of photographs and liberal use of images from space and historic or modern maps, bring us close to the action.

Despite a half century in exploration, How Man does not grow old in spirit. His curiosity remains that of a young explorer. His enthusiasm is infectious. His delight in the richness of geography and culture reminds us that true beauty is to be found in diversity.

George Yeo & HM / 楊榮文（右）& HM

It was my good luck to know How Man after re-locating to work in Hong Kong. His reputation preceded him. I like to think we are kindred spirits although, despite being younger, I lack his physical energy or courage. An evening with him is always a pleasure and an education.

How Man inspires not by preaching or argument, but by perspective. Somehow the same reality seen through his lenses appears more interesting, joyous and hopeful. This is a perspective the world sorely needs today. Hong Kong University's decision to name a centre after How Man in order to inspire others to follow in his footsteps is indeed farsighted. It is all too easy to fixate on the negative in the world and see the problem in other human beings. A change in perspective enables us to see the beauty in nature and the beauty of man in nature. Enlightened Sojourn enriches us in this way.

序

新加坡前外交部長 楊榮文

《齊物逍遙》在我心中是一部令人心蕩神馳的珍藏品，這個系列匯集了黃效文先生過去五十年來探險工作的實地報告，而這本書凝結了他近期旅程的精華。

永遠不要懷疑他講故事的能力，因為他的文字總是那麼引人入勝。透過他的敘述，我們得以共用他在世界各地的奇妙經歷。這些經歷是我夢寐以求但往往難以實現的，因為他們太偏離常軌，那些與之產生聯繫的人物，我彷彿只能在書中才能和其相遇。同時，書中那些精心挑選的照片，結合大量使用的衛星影像以及古今地圖，讓我們彷彿置身於那些生動的場景中，能近距離感受那分真實的震撼。

儘管半個世紀的探險生涯已匆匆過去，黃效文先生依然保持著旺盛的好奇心和極具感染力的熱情。他對地理和文化的追求提醒著我們，真正的美麗存在於多樣性之中。他是真正具有探險精神的人。

能夠認識黃效文先生是我的幸運。早在我搬到香港工作之前，就久聞他的盛名。我們有著志同道合的靈魂，儘管我比他年輕，卻缺乏他的精力與勇氣。每個能與他坐下來交談的夜晚都是那麼愉快又充滿教育意義。

黃效文先生對我的啟發並非來自說教的言詞或是銳利的辯論，而是來自他看待這個世界的視角。透過他的鏡頭，我能看到原本千篇一律的現實世界變得更加有趣、令人愉悅並且充滿希望。這正是當今世界迫切需要的視野。

香港大學決定以黃效文先生的名字命名一個探險交流中心，確實是高瞻遠矚的決策。不斷變化的社會環境迫使現在的人太容易執著於負面，並將問題歸咎他人。黃效文先生的精神能激勵我們追隨他的腳步，轉變視角，從而看到自然本身的美麗和身處自然中的人類所散發的人性美。《齊物逍遙》正是以這種方式啟迪了我們的心靈。

Preface

This special series of books, all with the same title of Enlightened Sojourn, is now into its sixth and seventh volume. They recount my travels and reflections. In the past, it used to come out as one book per year. With my waning years in energy and thus travel frequency, I expected that it would ultimately take two years of sojourn to compile one book, enlightened or not.

But not quite. Suddenly I found that after the pandemic, and four rounds of quarantine during that period in order to continue my fieldwork, I am squeezing more and more time to get into the field. It is as if I am trying to make up for time lost, as well as packing in as much field time as possible while counting down toward my own expiration date and lapsing eventually into obscurity.

Whatever reasons they may be, the sojourn for last year ended up not necessarily the most productive, yet resulting in a very diverse coverage in both latitude and longitude. As one volume, it would be way too long for a small-format book. Thus it is decided to split it into two books, Book 1 and Book 2, which I present herewith for my friends, supporters, and select readers.

Perhaps it is worth mentioning that I have often felt I am writing for myself, as a reminiscence and record of my own life and experience. If by chance it is read and appreciated by others, all the better. But I have never intended it as a popular publication for the mass market.

The illustrations, through images that I took, are often prompters to remind me of what I may want to write about. In some ways, I did not take pictures with my eyes, but my mind. That is a tradition and practice I have devised as my own style, and followed as early as during my stint at the National Geographic some forty years ago. It has served me well. As whatever dramatic experience I have encountered, I seem to have the picture to illustrate it, as fact rather than fiction.

I hope my readers would enjoy the stories as much as I would reminiscence these experiences, trivial as some may be.

前言

《齊物逍遙》這一系列特別書籍，現已進入第六本和第七本。這些書記載了我多年來的經歷與反思。過去，我每年都會出版一本書。然而隨著年事漸高，精力和旅行頻率逐漸減少，我原以為現階段完成一本書至少需要兩年的時間。

但事實是，疫情期間，我經歷了四次隔離，以期繼續做野外工作。這讓我愈發感慨時間的寶貴。於是疫情後，我開始更加努力地擠出時間進行野外工作，彌補失去的時光。生命的終點任何人都無法預測和左右，我只想在還能工作的日子裡，盡可能多地進行實地探索。

去年一整年的旅程雖然並非最具成效，但在緯度和經度上卻涵蓋了非常廣泛而多樣的範圍。若將其合併成一本書，會顯得過於冗長。因此，我決定將其分為兩本，即上下兩集，呈獻給我的朋友、支持者和精選的讀者們。

我常覺得我是在為自己而寫作，過程像在給自己留下一把回憶的鑰匙。如果這些文字偶然被他人閱讀並欣賞，那自然是極好的，但我從未打算將大眾市場的流行度作為衡量我作品的標準和追求。

每次我按下快門時，並非是用眼睛在拍照，而是在用我的頭腦和心靈。這就是為什麼我時常是先翻到照片，再開始寫文字。書中的那些圖像，常常會提醒我想要表達什麼。這是我在四十年前於美國《國家地理雜誌》工作時期便養成的習慣，一直以來對我幫助良多。無論我經歷了多麼戲劇性的事情，似乎總有影像來佐證這些經歷的絕對真實。

儘管本書中可能存在大量瑣碎的細節，但我仍希望讀者能夠像我回憶這些經歷時一樣，享受並從中解讀出積極的意義。

目次

卡
珠
修
道
院

KHARCHU GOMBA

Lhodrak, Tibet – June 7, 2023

KHARCHU GOMBA
A Tibetan monastery bordering Bhutan

Kharchu Gomba is an important Nyingma (Red Sect) monastery founded in 1570, over 450 years ago, at an altitude of over 4000 meters above sea level. The mountain on which it sits boasts over a hundred meditation caves, and Guru Rinpoche who brought Buddhism from India into Tibet is said to have meditated here for seven years during the 7th century.

This is the closest monastery to the Bhutan border. Before the pandemic, there were regular exchanges of trade and pilgrims visiting. During the summer the Bhutanese would cross by the high herding pasture pass to come here, and in winter they would follow a river that flows down from across the border into Tibet through a deep valley. Traditional merchandise were grain, electrical appliances, red salt, woven fabric, tea and wooden bowls. The last three were what Bhutanese across the border were famous for and used for exchange.

The government recently built a paved road which ends at the monastery, not only for the convenience of pilgrims but also hoping to attract tourists. But the monastery attracts also something far more unique and special. As soon as we park our cars, I see two dark, sharp-horned, mountain goats grazing peacefully along the guard rail of the road. These animals are known to be

Shampa Tsumdrup / 本寺住持   Entrance to monastery / 寺院大門

very alert and shy, but here they seem totally at peace.

We stay the night at the monastery and are served a rather simple meal by the attending monks. There is still some construction going on in the courtyard, as it seems the monastery is gearing up to accommodate a sudden flood of visitors. Behind the monastery, the hill drops down to a flush wooded valley and there are occasional chortens and pagodas dotting the otherwise green overgrowth. Prayer flags mark a few trails where pilgrims go about their circumambulation of the nearby mountain.

The next morning, I want to pay a visit to the head monk. Before I enter the main premises, I come face to face with the most beautiful pheasant I have ever seen. Its head is like that of a peacock and the body sports a rainbow of colors, shining all the way to the tail. This is the rare Himalayan Monal (Lophophorus impejanus), Red-listed as

Snow peaks around monastery / 寺院周圍積雪的山頂

globally Endangered and the national bird of Nepal. A rainbow has seven shades of color, but this pheasant is said to have nine, thus the local name of "Nine Colored Bird". Perhaps his silver and gold taints are considered the two additional colors.

This single bird is casually feeding on some barley grain that I suppose the monks have laid out by the entrance door. He - as the attractive colors are reserved for male birds - ignores my presence and continues to nip away leisurely.

Nine-colored Bird / 傳説中的九色鳥

Suddenly, a mother and child mountain goat also appear. I cannot tell if they are serow or goral or tahr, and only later find out that they are Himalayan Goral (Naemorhedus goral), a species that occurs in China only at a few spots. They too are coming by for their breakfast alongside the pheasant. The two beautiful species, one a bird the other a mammal, share the meal and the space quietly as if neighbors cohabiting a common home. The setting is so tranquil that I sit there for a long moment to just absorb the peace and serenity. Such moments are therapeutic beyond what any mind-healing gurus can offer.

One such guru is 43 year old Shampa Tsumdrup who lives just beyond the door inside the monastery. He is the head monk of Kharchu Monastery, *where today there are 34 monks in total. His CV is quite impressive, including studies at some of the most important scholastic centers on the plateau. Coming from a livestock-tending family of nearby Lakhang town, he was influenced by Buddhist activities of the monastery from an early age and wanted to become a monk. His parents gave consent when he was twelve years old, so he entered Kharchu Monastery as a novice.*

Shampa later studied under Buddhist masters at Samye Monastery, the oldest established monastery of Tibet, founded in the 8th Century. From there he went on to Baiyu Monastery for two additional years of study, before heading in 2006 to Beijing to join the Tibetan Buddhist

Himalayan Monal / 棕尾虹雉   Himalayan Monal and Gorels / 棕尾虹雉和牠的斑羚朋友們

Academy for two years. Upon graduating as a khenpo, the highest degree in Nyingma Buddhism, equivalent to a PhD in the West, Shampa returned to Kharchu Monastery to become its head. Recently, he published a book regarding the history of his home monastery and the adjacent meditation legacy.

Shampa hosts us in his private chamber, almost as colorful as the Himalayan Monal. He is very soft spoken and humble, matching his kind face. As gifts, he gives us special tea picked at lower elevations of the mountain, some blessed pills for all ailments, the book he wrote in Tibetan, and for me a special tiny statue of a deity of his Nyingma Sect.

Before the new road was finished during the pandemic, the monastery is not known beyond its immediate vicinity and then mainly among Tibetan pilgrims. But the situation may soon change with today's internet age. It can be expected that the many independent tourists will soon be heading up to this remote corner of China next to Bhutan.

With this new influx of visitors, the monastery will likely receive more supplicant donations. But I hope at the same time, the lovely wildlife, like the "Nine-Colored Bird" and its neighbours the gorals, would also multiply and continue to thrive on this peaceful border.

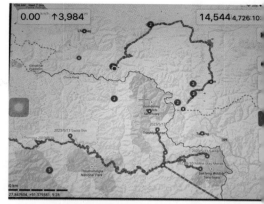

Kharchu Gomba by Bhutan border route map /
不丹邊境路線圖上呈現的卡珠寺
Kharchu Monastery plaque / 卡珠寺牌

卡珠修道院

鄰接不丹的西藏寺廟

卡珠修道院是一座源遠流長的寧瑪派（紅教）寺院，於一五七〇年建立，至今歷史已超過四百五十年。它坐落於海拔高達四千米的雄偉山巒之巔，山上擁有百餘座禪修洞窟。傳說西元七世紀，蓮花生大師從印度傳佛法至西藏時，曾在此冥思七載。

這是最接近不丹邊境的寺院。疫情前，常有貿易客和朝聖者往來。夏季，不丹人會越過高山牧地來此，冬日則沿著一條從邊境流入西藏的深谷河流前來。傳統的貿易物品包括糧食、電器、紅鹽、織物、茶葉和木碗。後三者是不丹邊境進口最流行的交換品。

政府近期修築了一條通往寺院的柏油路，不只方便了朝聖者，也期望能吸引遊客。但這座寺院吸引的，好像還有更特別的東西。比如現在，我們剛停好車，就看到兩隻深色尖角的山羊，在路邊護欄旁悠閒地吃草。這些動物向來警覺怕羞，但在這裡，牠們看起來彷彿完全無憂。

我們在寺院過夜，僧侶們供應了一頓簡單的晚餐。院子裡仍在不停歇地施工，似乎在為突如其來的遊客潮做準備。寺院後方，山坡下至一片綠意盎然的樹林谷地，偶然能見到有些零星的佛塔點綴在綠色植被中。經幡標識著幾條小徑，有朝聖者正沿著標識轉山。

翌日清晨，我正準備去拜訪一下寺院的住持，美好的相遇就在此刻發生。我踏入正殿之前，一隻我生平見過的最華美的雉雞正在大殿門口啄食麥粒。牠的頭部宛如孔雀，身軀則披著斑斕的彩虹，光彩奪目，一直綻放至尾端。這便是罕見的棕尾虹雉，被列為全球瀕危物種，還是尼泊爾的國鳥。彩虹有七色，但據說這雉雞擁有九色，因此當地人稱之為「九色鳥」。或許牠的金銀兩色斑點被視為額外的兩色吧。

從色彩斑斕的毛色便能看出這是一個「靚仔」。可能帥哥之間也存在攀比心，所以當我靠近牠時，牠裝作對我的存在視而不見，相當漠然，繼續悠然自得地啄食。

突然，一對山羊母子也出現了。我無法分辨牠們是長鬚羚還是斑羚或塔爾羊，後來才得知牠們是喜馬拉雅斑羚，只生活於中國境內極少數地方。牠們同樣是前來享用早餐的，與前面那位「靚仔」肩並肩。此刻，鳥類和哺乳動物兩個不同的物種就像親切的鄰居一樣共處一個和諧的家園。這一幕是如此的可愛，我在那裡久坐，只為多吸收一會兒這分平和與寧靜。於我而言，這樣的時刻，其治愈效果是不管多厲害的心靈治療大師都沒法企及的。

A mountain goat / 悠閒的山羊
Blue sheep at gate / 寺門岩羊

其實這裡就有一位大師，四十三歲的山帕·增卓，他是卡珠寺的住持，寺院目前共有三十四名僧人。山帕曾在高原上幾所地位最

Shampa with HM / 住持與 HM

Main assembly hall / 誦經大廳

高的學術中心進修，而他整體的履歷也相當令人印象深刻。他出身於附近拉康鎮的一個放牧家庭，自幼便受到寺院佛教活動的影響，渴望成為一名僧侶。十二歲時，經過父母同意後，他以沙彌，也就是小學徒的身分進入了卡珠寺。

後來，山帕又有機會師從西藏最古老的寺院，桑耶寺中的佛教大師們。那之後，他在四川甘孜規模龐大的白玉寺進修了兩年，又於二〇〇六年前往北京加入藏傳佛教學院，研習了兩年。畢業後，他取得了寧瑪派的最高學位，堪布，相當於西方的博士學位。最後，山帕返回卡珠寺，成為了寺院的主持。最近，他還出版了一本關於卡珠寺歷史及相關禪修文化的書籍。

山帕住持在他自己的房間接待了我們，其色彩繽紛程度不亞於剛才那隻棕尾虹雉。他面相慈祥和善，說話溫和謙遜，讓我想到一個成語，相由心生。他還送了我們很多特別的禮物，比如在山腳下採摘的特殊茶葉，一些加持過的據說可治百病的藥丸以及他用藏語寫的書。還有一份獨屬於我的小禮物，是一尊寧瑪派神祇的微型雕像。

在疫情期間，新道路完工之前，這座寺院除了藏族朝聖者外，鮮為人知。但在當今網際網絡時代，我想情況可能很快就會改變。或許不久的將來就會有很多背包客出現在這個毗鄰不丹的中國偏遠角落。

有了這些遊客的湧入，寺院應該能收到更多的香客捐獻。但我同時也希望，像九色鳥以及牠的鄰居斑羚們這樣可愛的野生動物，能夠在瞬息萬變的現代社會中不被干擾，繼續在這片和平的邊境繁衍生息，茁壯成長。

Chorten & pagoda / 中土與西藏風格的寶塔
Pilgrimage route / 朝聖山徑

西藏南部的夏爾巴人

THE SHERPA AND THEIR COMMUNITY IN CHINA

Zhenthang, Tibet – June 10, 2023

THE SHERPA AND THEIR COMMUNITY IN CHINA

Sherpa is a Tibetan word, meaning people of the East, or from the east. Legend has it that they migrated long ago from the Kham area in the eastern part of the Tibetan plateau. That is today's western Sichuan and easternmost TAR, which is home to the Khampa, a most gallant subgroup among Tibetan people. They are famous as the stockiest, fiercest, most warrior-like, and bravest of the plateau. So it is not unfitting that the Sherpa, like the Khampa, are brave and persevering, though not in a martial sense.

The Sherpa, over time, have become a distinct group of Tibetan people residing mainly on the southern slopes of the Himalayas. They concentrate along the foothill border belt of today's Nepal with a population of around half a million. But a few little-known pockets of Sherpa villages and communities still inhabit north of the range, on the Tibetan side within China, where I am now.

The Sherpa's culture, history and religion are largely aligned with that of the Tibetan nomads on the plateau, though in lifestyle they have transitioned from being nomadic livestock herders to transhumance pastoralists, tending to high mountain yak and sheep, but also cultivating terraced fields at lower elevation with marginal and subsistence farming.

Hillary climbing in front of Tenzing / 希拉里攀爬在丹增前面

The Sherpa people, as an ethnic group, have gained the notice and recognition of the West, as well as the world over, within the last hundred years. They have become by far the most notable group in mountaineering history and a legacy of the Himalayas. It is no exaggeration to say that, without the Sherpa, modern mountaineering history would be nearly wiped out, if not completely so. The physically challenging endeavor of high-altitude climbing would never have become such a hotly pursued sport without the involvement and support of the Sherpa.

The defining moment for the Sherpa was on May 29, 1953 when Tenzing Norgay became one of first two men to set foot on Everest, highest mountain in the world. He and Edmund Hillary, a beekeeper from New Zealand, made mountaineering history with this crowning achievement. The humble and modest Sherpa, who was quickly claimed by both Nepal and India as their native son, did not look at this as a conquest, but as a blessing from

Tenzing & his mother / 丹增與他的母親

Qomolongma, the female goddess who is the source of the traditional name for Everest. She had shown pity on him, thus allowing him to reach the top. This is a sharp contrast to what his climbing mate Edmund Hillary cracked upon his descent to the South Col support camp: "We knocked the bastard off!" Hillary, later on in life, were to redeem his arrogance by devoting much of his life by returning his service to the Sherpa.

Tenzing's modesty would set the model for many male and female Sherpa mountaineers to follow, overcoming the utmost physical challenges with inward mental and spiritual balance. Sherpa achievements at global summits are too long to list, and it would make leading climbers of other nations pale in comparison. Not to mention the supply chain run by the Sherpa, who handle all the climbing logistics, shuttling supplies and equipment in long human caravans to multiple high camps throughout the Himalayas. Their activities include emergency evacuation of climbers from thin air back to the safety of basecamps, a life-threatening endeavor even for the best among climbers.

Some quotes regarding Tenzing, the best-known of all Sherpas, would be appropriate here. "There is a flame in Tenzing, a marvelously strong and pure flame that no storm of man or nature can extinguish. It is compounded of dream and desire, will and struggle, pride and humility;

and in the end, with the deed done, the victory gained, it is the man's humility that stands out above all his other qualities. In his moment of triumph what he felt in his heart was gratitude to Everest. His prayer for his future life is that it may be worthy of Everest..." *(James Ramsey Ullman, Tiger of the Snows)*

I happen to know Tenzing's eldest son Norbu and youngest son Dhamey quotes his father: "You cannot be a good mountaineer, however great your ability, unless you are cheerful and have the spirit of comradeship. Friends are as important as achievement...teamwork is the one key to success, and selfishness only makes a man small. No man, on a mountain or elsewhere, gets more out of anything than he puts into it. Be Great, Make Others Great."

Dhamey sent me a photo of himself as a young boy of five, taken at around 1975, when he received his first pair of mountaineering boots from his father. The picture shows the kid on one knee while his father bends down to tie his laces. From a Sherpa son about his Sherpa father in his own words : "To me, the man behind the mask atop Everest was my Pala, the Sherpa and Tibetan word for father. I am the youngest son of Tenzing and was born long after his Everest ascent. In many ways I feel fortunate to be born after Everest. I got to know the other side of Tenzing, a fantastic regular dad – funny at times, humble and one who gave us his complete affection." Today, Dhamey puts his time and effort not into climbing, but into working for the betterment, welfare and respect due the Sherpa people. As with his father, Tenzing Norgay not only broke the snow path to the summit of Everest, he also broke the stereotyped path for the entire Sherpa community, gaining them fame, recognition and respect.

With this background of the Sherpa, my team and I penetrated the Tibet/Nepal border to Zhenthang, where six Sherpa villages exist hidden in a forest sanctuary of the Himalayas. In these villages there are around 400 households with a little over 2000 people, of which 99% are Sherpa. "Thang" in Tibetan is a place name, like

Sherpa houses at Xuezongma / 雪雄瑪村裡的夏爾巴人房屋

Lithang, Bathang, Gyalthang (known as Shangri-la today) - all in the Kham area. So Zhenthang's name may have originated from its association with people from Kham as well. We headed to the furthest village of Xuezongma, one that has two hot springs nearby.

While visiting one of the hot springs, we ran into a father and daughter also heading there and gave them a ride. Norbu the father is 34 and the daughter Laba is 13. Together with Laba's four sisters, they move to high camp every summer to tend to their livestock. During the winter, they stay at their winter home. Since 2017, each Sherpa family has been assigned a new home built by the government, besides receiving Rmb 3000 per person as annual subsidy.

Before the pandemic, each year during the summer and autumn, the family would hire a few Sherpa workers from across the border in Nepal to come help in farm work. On top of providing meals and accommodations in their home, they would have to pay the workers Rmb 200 per day. Each time the workers would stay for five days, twice a year for a total of ten days. At Zhenthang, some Nepali Sherpa workers stayed behind and married into a local Sherpa family becoming localized.

Nanji is 66 years old. Compared to other Sherpa, he is widely traveled and

Nanji with his drum & hunting spear /
南傑與他的鼓和狩獵長矛
Sherpa young mother with baby /
年輕的夏爾巴媽媽與她的小孩

has been throughout different regions of the plateau, including Amdo to the northeast, Kham to the east, and of course Lhasa. With a pig tail hanging down his back, beaded necklace and felt hat, he looks more Tibetan than the usual Sherpa. Indeed Sherpa are of Tibetan stock. Even Tenzing Norgay, the mountaineering hero, admitted late in life that he was born and grew up on the Tibet side of the border valley.

Nanji is a very handy person, showing us a wooden drum with yak hide that he made. He uses it to perform religious ceremonies for the villagers, like a local shaman. When there are disputes within the village, he takes the role of "Ah Ya" and becomes the arbitrator as well as the judge. Recently, he received a contract to transport cement, bricks and mortar from the road to the famous Nine Eyes Hot Spring an hour away. The local government is eager to turn that into a tourist site. On each trip, he could carry 30 to 35 kilos of material at Rmb two Yuan per kilo. Each day he can haul a load twice, netting a monthly income of between 3000 to 4500 Rmb, sufficient to feed his family of seven.

Another work for income is the collecting of cordyceps and the making of "Ji Zhua Gu" liquor from a local grain with seed-heads shaped a little like chicken feet. Between the months of May to July, the entire family goes to high country to collect cordyceps, the medicinal fungus-infected worm. Though this region is not best known for cordyceps, each piece can still fetch between Rmb 10 and 18 Yuan. On average, each month they can net about 1000 pieces, making a good addition to their other farming income. During the leisure months, the wife Lamo also weaves some bamboo baskets for sale to supplement their income. The baby-carrying basket is quite unique, being strapped over the forehead with a chord, with the basket set in a sideways fashion on the back. We collected a number of woven products including one baby carrier for the CERS collection.

The special grain liquor is said to become more mellow as it ages. We had the opportunity to try some, served inside a bamboo tube with a straw through which to suck it. It is said that the locals compare the vintage liquor to the amniotic fluid of a pregnant woman. It is a reflection of the early worship of a woman's reproductive power, remnant of the respect for the female during the early matrilineal period in Tibetan history.

Our visit to the Sherpa villages of China may have been short, but it filled a gap among my almost fifty years of work on minorities of China. For now, the Sherpa are not recognized as a separate entity within China's minority nationalities but are considered a subgroup of the Tibetans. Sherpa status and renown however have grown far beyond these hidden mountains and valleys of the Himalayas, and their achievements have landed them in the vocabulary of the world with worthy admiration. No wonder Dhamey is so proud of his father Tenzing Norgay. The world should be, too.

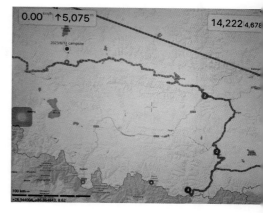

Route to Zhenthang at border point 4 /
在 4 號邊界前往陳塘鎮的路線

西藏南部的夏爾巴人

「夏爾巴」在藏語中被意為東方人或來自東方的人。傳說很久以前,夏爾巴人從青藏高原東部的康巴地區遷移到西藏的山南地區。歷史上的康巴人作為西藏部落中最為勇猛的一支,曾分布於今天西藏的最東部和四川的西部地區,因此這一地區也被人稱之為是康巴人的家園。康巴人體型健碩,通常被認為是高原上最強壯、最兇猛和最勇敢部落的後裔。因此,夏爾巴人和康巴人一樣,勇敢而堅韌不拔,雖然並不指在武力與打鬥意義上。

如今,夏爾巴人已經成為主要居住在喜馬拉雅山脈南麓的一個獨特的藏民族的分支。他們集中居住在今天尼泊爾山麓的邊界地區,人口約為五十萬。但是在中國境內的西藏,一些鮮為人知的夏爾巴人的村莊和社區仍坐落在喜馬拉雅山脈以北的地區,也就是我現在所在的地方。

夏爾巴人的文化、歷史和宗教在很大程度上都與居住在青藏高原上的西藏遊牧民族保持著一致。儘管在生活方式上,夏爾巴人已經從純粹的遊牧民族轉變為半農半牧的民族,透過在高原上放犛牛和綿羊,以及在一些低海拔的梯田上種植少量的農作物維持生計。

而夏爾巴人作為一個民族，在近一百年的時間裡，陸續得到了西方國家乃至整個世界的認可和關注。截至目前，他們已經成為了世界登山史上最負盛名的一個群組，也成為了喜馬拉雅山脈不得不提的標誌性人物和符號。毫不誇張地說，如果沒有夏爾巴人，現代登山運動的歷史將會被重新改寫或消失，亦或被全部抹去。如果沒有夏爾巴人的積極參與和堅守，高海拔攀登這項對身體有著極致挑戰和嚴苛要求的運動，將永遠不會受到大眾如此熱烈的追捧和歡迎。

對於夏爾巴人來說，一九五三年五月二十九日是一個值得被紀念和具有歷史意義的一天。丹增・諾蓋（*Tenzing Norgay*），一個出生在喜馬拉雅南西藏和尼泊爾邊境的夏爾巴人，成為了歷史上最早登上世界最高峰珠穆朗瑪峰的兩個人之一。他和來自紐西蘭的養蜂人艾德蒙・希拉里（*Edmund Hillary*），憑藉這一至高的成就創造了世界登山史的記錄。這之後，這位謙遜、憨厚的夏爾巴人很快被尼泊爾和印度政府認領，稱其為自己本國的兒子（公民）。然而年輕的丹增・諾蓋並不認為這次登山的勝利是對大自然的征服，相反，他認為這次勝利是珠穆朗瑪女神對他們的祝福和庇佑。因為珠穆朗瑪女神的加持和慈悲，才得以讓丹增・諾蓋和他的夥伴成功登上了山頂。這與他的夥伴艾德蒙・希拉里（*Edmund Hillary*）下山後的反應形成了鮮明的對比。艾德蒙下山後說道：「我們把那混蛋打倒了！」

Climbing team with Sherpa in front /
夏爾巴人與登山團隊
A Sherpa with Nepalese money /
夏爾巴人展示尼泊爾紙鈔

Tenzing on Everest summit /
登頂珠穆朗瑪峰的丹增

丹增的謙遜無疑為這之後許許多多的夏爾巴人樹立了良好的榜樣，透過內在的修行和精神的平衡克服身體的挑戰成為了夏爾巴人克服高山險阻不變的信條和宗旨。如今，夏爾巴人在全球登山界取得的成績太過耀眼，如一一例舉，恐怕會讓那些其他國家的登山隊員們感到慚愧和自愧不如。更不用說由夏爾巴人管理和實踐的有關高峰攀岩的一系列供應鏈服務，其中不僅包括了所有登山所需的後勤保障、物資運輸，以及人力扛運登山的裝備和設備到喜馬拉雅山脈多個高海拔的登山營地，還包括了將登山者從稀薄的空氣中緊急疏散到大本營的救援活動，這項任務即使對最優秀的登山者來說，都是一項危及生命的高危活動。

在這裡，我想引用一句描述夏爾巴人丹增・諾蓋的著名節錄：「丹增身上有一種熊熊不滅的火焰，那是一種不可思議的、強烈的和純淨的火焰，任何風暴或自然都無法將它熄滅。它是夢想與渴望、意志與奮鬥、驕傲與謙卑的結合體。最後，隨著行動的完成，勝利的獲得，這個人的謙遜比他所有的品質都要突出。在他勝利的那一刻，他內心的感受是對珠穆朗瑪峰的感激。而他對於未來生活的祈禱是，他此後的這一生都能夠配得上那座神聖的珠穆朗瑪峰……」（《雪之虎》詹姆斯・拉姆齊・烏爾曼）

機緣巧合之下，我正好也跟丹增・諾蓋的大兒子諾布和小兒子達米相識。根據他們的描述，父親曾說過：「無論你的能力有多大，如果不能保持心情愉悅且具備良好的團隊精神，你就永遠不能成為一名好登山運動員。在登山領域，朋友和成就是同等的重要。團隊合作是成功的關鍵，自私只會讓人變得渺小。無論是在山上還是在別的地方，沒有人能從任何事情中得到比他投入得到的更多的東西。成為偉大的人，要讓別人也變得偉大。」

達米曾給我發過一張他五歲時的照片。照片拍攝於一九七五年左右，當時他剛從父親那裡收到了他的第一雙登山靴。照片上他單膝跪地，父親正彎腰給他繫著鞋帶。達米說道：「對我來說，珠峰上那個戴著面具的男人就是我的帕拉（夏爾巴語和藏語中父親的意思）。我是丹增最小的兒子，在他登上珠穆朗瑪峰很久之後出生。從很多方面，我都覺得自己很幸運能夠出生在他登上珠穆朗瑪峰之後。這使我瞭解到了他的另一面，他是一個非常出色，也很普通的父親——幽默、謙遜，並且給了我們他全部的愛。」這是來自一個夏爾巴兒子對自己夏爾巴父親的表述和獨白。現在，達米並沒有子承父業，將自己的時間和精力都用於攀登。相反的，他的事業是為夏爾巴人提供更好的生活、福利和尊重。這一點和他的父親一樣，丹增·諾蓋在自己的職業生涯中，不僅開闢了通往珠穆朗瑪峰頂峰的雪道，也在世界舞臺上打破了大眾對於夏爾巴人的刻板印象，為他們贏得了名聲、認可和尊重。

有了這些與夏爾巴人的聯繫與淵源，我和我的團隊穿過西藏和尼

Tenzing tying Dhamey's boots /
丹增正在幫達米繫鞋帶
Sherpa father & baby / 夏爾巴父親與小嬰兒

泊爾的邊境地區，來到了隱藏在喜馬拉雅森林保護區的六個夏爾巴村落。這些村子大約有四百戶人家，共兩千多人，其中百分之九十九是夏爾巴人。「塘」在藏語中是一個地名，如藏區的理塘、巴塘、建塘（即今天的香格里拉）等地區，這些都位於西藏東部的康巴地區。因此，陳塘的名字很可能也源於與它相關聯的東部康巴人。我們團隊沿著這條線，一路走到了陳塘鎮最遠的，有著兩個天然溫泉的雪雄瑪村。

在參觀雪雄瑪村其中的一個溫泉時，我們在路上偶遇了一對夏爾巴父女。他們當時正徒步前往村裡的九眼溫泉，我們順路便載了他們一程。父親羅布今年三十四歲，女兒拉巴十三歲。每年夏天，拉巴和四個姊妹會一起搬到自家的高山夏季牧場去放牧，照看牲畜。而在冬天，他們則待在陳塘鎮的家裡過冬。自二〇一七年以來，政府為陳塘鎮每一戶夏爾巴家庭修建了新房，而且每人每年還可以收到三千元的生活補貼。

在疫情之前，每年的夏季和秋季，羅布都會從尼泊爾邊境的另一邊雇傭一些夏爾巴人到自家的農田裡幹農活。除了為他們提供食宿以外，每人每天還會得到二百元人民幣的薪酬。陳塘鎮的農田是一年兩熟，所以工人們每年會來兩次，每次停留五天左右的時間。在陳塘鎮，有些尼泊爾的夏爾巴人則選擇留了下來，與當地人結婚並組成家庭，在當地定居和生活。

南傑今年六十六歲，與陳塘鎮的其他夏爾巴人相比，他遊歷廣泛，去過藏區包括東北部的安多、東部的康區，還有拉薩等許多地方。他頭上編著一條小辮，自然地垂在他身後。我看他手上佩戴的佛珠和頭上的羊毛氈帽，覺得他比一般的夏爾巴人看著更像是藏族人。事實上，夏爾巴人也是藏族人的一部分，就連登山英雄丹增·諾蓋（*Tenzing*

Sherpa woman with headdress / 戴頭飾的夏爾巴女人
Sherpa baby basket collected / 收集的夏爾巴嬰兒背籃

Norgay）在晚年的時候也曾承認，他出生並成長在邊境山谷的西藏一側。

南傑是一個手藝靈巧的夏爾巴人，在他居住的小木屋，他向我們展示了他用犛牛皮製作的木鼓。每當村裡舉行節日或祭祀的時候，他都會用木鼓為村民舉行一些宗教的儀式，就像當地的薩滿一樣。當村裡發生糾紛時，他則會扮演成「阿亞」的角色，成為仲裁者和法官。最近，他接到了一份合約，是將水泥、磚塊和砂漿從雪雄瑪村山下的小路上運送到一小時腳程外的九眼溫泉處。當地政府急於把這個溫泉打造成一個旅遊景點，所以南傑每天便往返於兩點之間，以每公斤兩元的價格搬運三十到三十五公斤的材料到山上再折返。每天，南傑可以來回搬運兩趟，每月獲得三千到四千五百元的收入，足以養活他的七口之家。

在雪雄瑪村，另一個比較賺錢的工種是採集冬蟲草，還有用雞爪穀釀製「雞爪穀」酒。每年五月到七月之間，雪雄瑪村的村民桑布一家都會全家人出動到山上採集冬蟲草。雖然這個地區的冬蟲夏草算不上很出名，但每根還是可以賣到十到十八元的價格。平均每個月，桑布一家每人可以淨賺大約一千塊，相比於村裡其他的農業收入來說，這是一個很可觀的增加收入方式。在閒暇的時候，桑布的妻子拉姆也會用當地的藤條編織一些竹籃進行出售，以補充家裡的收入。夏爾巴人背著嬰兒的籃子也非常的獨特，是用一塊布條頂在額頭上，然後將籃子背在身體的背部。我們這次考察的途中，也收集了一些編織的產品，其中就包括一個嬰兒背籃。

據介紹，夏爾巴人的這種特殊的雞爪穀酒經過發酵後會變得越來越醇厚。學會的工作人員訪問一戶人家時，我們也有機會嘗試了一下，酒是用竹筒盛著，然後插入一根竹子做的吸管開始吮吸。據說，當地的夏爾巴人會把這種陳年雞爪穀酒比作孕婦的羊水，反映了早期夏爾巴人對女性生殖能力的崇拜，也印證西藏歷史上早期母系社會時期對女性尊崇的殘餘。

我們對中國夏爾巴人村莊的訪問可能很短，但它填補了我近五十年來研究中國少數民族的空白。目前，夏爾巴人還不被承認為是中國少數民族中的一個獨立的群體，僅被認為是藏族的一個分支。然而，夏爾巴人的地位和名聲卻遠遠超出了喜馬拉雅山脈的這些隱蔽的山脈和山谷，他們的成就使他們在世界舞臺上獲得了值得欽佩的地位。難怪達米會對他的父親丹增·諾蓋感到如此的驕傲和自豪，其實世人也應該如此。

Sherpa home-brewed liquor / 夏爾巴人自釀的酒

從西藏到新疆（上）

TIBET BY A NEW ROAD INTO XINJIANG (Part 1)

Dunhuang, Gansu – June 23, 2023

TIBET BY A NEW ROAD INTO XINJIANG (Part 1)

It is not easy to get a listing in the Guinness Book of World Records. But Dagejia Geyser has its place firmly fixed as the highest active geyser and geothermal field in the world, at an elevation of approximately 5100 meters above sea level.

The field is not just a number of hot pools; it encompasses the most powerful geyser field in Asia. With adjacent thermal springs bubbling, they number over a hundred and extend over an area of one kilometer in distance. Some twenty of these hot spring fountains are true geysers, periodically erupting with water and steam and then going into a period of silence. These are the Old Faithful of Tibet, similar to the famous geyser at Yellowstone National Park in the western USA. One of the largest geysers has an interval of some three hours of sleep before waking up again. The others may have a cycle of ten-minute eruptions followed by periods of over a day of quiet. The spewed-out column of boiling water can be as high as seven to eight meters in height.

I spent some time with the largest spring. Every now and then, it would explode and erupt with overheated groundwater, simultaneously letting out a cloud of hot steam into the cold air of Tibet. It would then bubble in dormancy for up to ten minutes before repeating the performance, releasing its powerful ejection to a height of twenty meters above an already dizzying elevation. The jet can

Dagejia Geyser Spring 2002 / 2002 年的搭各加噴泉

be up to two meters wide with a huge column of water being ejected. With each of its spewing and spraying, it would deposit a thin layer of cesium ore around the geyser. This has been repeated over centuries or millenniums.

I first visited the Degejia hot springs in 2002 after my circumambulation of Mount Kailash. Now over twenty years later, I have finally returned, as my team and I are on our way to cross from western Tibet into Xinjiang. We camp out next to one of the lesser hot springs, one at which the local Tibetans had managed to divert cold water from a nearby river to cool the steaming pool to bathing temperature. After soaking myself for a while in this medicinal spring, we visit one of our neighbors camping in a big tent.

Tseren Zeweng is 42 years of age. He came here in April to the hot spring to set up a sundry shop and restaurant inside the tent. It is mainly to serve Tibetans coming here from all over the Tibetan Plateau for the therapeutic baths. Each month, he can derive a meager profit of 2,000 RMB. Tseren tells us Dagejia is known to have 108 springs, and each has its own medicinal related value. Some are good for the liver, some for rheumatism, some for the heart, and some can be remedy for all ailments. One of the springs is believed to be where the legendary king Gesar's first wife Brugmo washed her hair.

Due to the pandemic, in these last couple years, the number of tourists to this site has dropped dramatically. But recently there seems to have been a gradual increase. Tibetan nomads will come around the months of July and August, and during the winter many will come set up camp and bathe for half a month or longer. The majority of them will come from Sakya and Ngamring Counties of Shigaze Prefecture, and Coqen County of Ngari Prefecture. From April on this year, each day may have had ten to twenty visitors arriving, though few would stay overnight.

The reason to pass through here is for our team to get to Gaize County in the north. Here is an area, the Qiangtang National Nature Reserve, that is by far the largest natural protected area in China, where multiple species of Tibetan wildlife roam free. There are flagship species like Wild Yak, Tibetan Antelope, Tibetan Wild Ass, Tibetan Gazelle, Tibetan Brown Bear and many other fauna of note.

The reserve covers an area of 334,000 square kilometers with its size in the league of Germany, Finland or Malaysia. The entire region is well above 4500 meters in altitude, with much above 5000 meters. Here is where a new road, National Highway 216, has just been completed, crossing over the prohibitive west Qiangtang Plateau and the eastern Karakoram Mountains into the basin

CERS team camp / 中國探險學會的露營地

of the Taklimakan Desert in Xinjiang. My intention is to take my time crossing this stretch of over 800 kilometers of wilderness before the wave of self-driving tourists should arrive. But it is not to be.

We arrive in Gaize early in the morning after camping out nearby. Going by this newly paved road requires getting a special permit to fill up jerry tanks for gasoline, as there is no gas station in between Tibet and Xinjiang. The doors to the government office open at 9 am, and there is a line of people already ahead of us. We get numbers 27 to 29 in line for our three cars, including one for my camper van. Surprise - no more numbers are given out after us, as the office will close at 12 noon and not open in the afternoon. There is a paper notice on the wall that the new road will be closed again as of tomorrow for major inspection. Ours will be the last batch of cars allowed through, and everyone must pass through the Tibet section of over 400 kilometers within the time period from afternoon to before midnight.

Team dining in camper van / 露營車中的集體晚餐

11th hour permit paper / 最後一刻的許可證

There are a few pickup trucks stacked high with new jerry cans in front of the office, opportunists or entrepreneurs who know about good merchandising. We quickly buy four cans for each car. We receive our permits in hand literally at the eleventh hour just as the office was ready to close. Rushing to the closest gas station, we fill up our cars and all the jerry cans. We hit the road without any thought of lunch. We are in a race with time, crossing a faraway provincial border before the road will be closed for indefinite days or weeks.

The newly paved road is smooth but the pristine scenery of the wild Tibetan plateau keeps the foot light on the accelerator. Meeting a deadline and countering an urge to stop and record the beautiful scenery becomes a constant battle in the mind. Often the bliss of nature overtakes my logical mind, which is arguing for discipline.

It is now passed the middle of June and the female Tibetan Antelope have started their migration to hidden calving ground deeps inside the mountains. We run into several such large herds and cannot help but stop to use our drones to follow them on their march. It is quite surprising that they will walk and stop to graze even as our drone is hovering above them to film, a sign that the last three decades of conservation efforts are coming to fruition.

Scenic Hwy 216 / 風光明媚的 216 號公路
Tibetan Wild Ass / 藏野驢

Male Tibetan Antelope in snow / 雪中公藏羚羊
Migrating Tibetan Antelope herd / 遷徙中的藏羚羊群

Scorched earth / 焦土區
Wild Yak / 野犛牛

With the Wild Ass, it is quite different, as scattered herds converge upon our approaching, and soon go into a gallop, at times becoming a stampede as the drone approaches. We only occasion upon Wild Yak one time and are only able to make a quick stop to take a couple of far - off photographs, as our time is running out. Pristine lakes with snow peaks around escort us like panoramic screens on both sides of our road until we reach an area with black rocks on both sides like torched earth with a backdrop of glaciated mountains. At such a prohibitive elevation, rain soon turns into hail and then snow, a welcome sight before descending into the dry hot desert.

We finally also go into a stampede as we cross a high pass where much snow is still covering both sides of the road. A sign by the roadside indicates that we are now crossing into Xinjiang, a spot that merits a group photo. Soon we will descend into what western media has been hyping as a territory of "concentration camps". Such biased and inaccurate reporting without consideration of context is losing the western media a lot of long-time friends, myself included. But I have been traveling in and out of Xinjiang since 1979 and have many local friends.

As I always say, talk is cheap. Looking into the eyes of a child or an old man will tell you a lot more. Unfortunately, sick air out of a bad mouth infected with real or imagined grievances, travels faster in this time and age for a *public salivating for dramatic stories. Each country's media ultimately serves its own political need. Some package it better than others. Done well, it is called Free Press; blunders are dismissed as propaganda. Unfortunately, I have to lament about such political pollutants while drowning in the wonderful sights bestowed by nature.*

With the well-constructed road, I wonder why they need to close the road for inspection. So what if it is for military logistics? That's a given for any country. We are well into Xinjiang before night fall as we see Tibetan Antelope marching up the mountain from the west. By then it is around 9 pm and the sky is still bright, naturally, given that Xinjiang is three time zones away from Beijing but keeps to the national time of the capital. The long downhill run is just as beautiful as the climb even though it is beginning to get dark. There were still some 300 kilometers to the town of Minfeng at the southern edge of the Taklimakan Desert.

There is an old saying in Xinjiang which suddenly becomes even more true as I descend from the high plateau to the depths of the second largest moving desert in the world. "Morning with thick coat, by noon in silk linen, hug a fire stove while eating watermelon," a reference to the dramatic climatic changes within hours. As an explorer, I am used to embracing the extremes. Traveling from Tibet into Xinjiang is one such manifestation.

從西藏到新疆（上）令人一見傾心的新路線

想要在金氏世界紀錄中留名，那可不是件輕而易舉的事。但搭各加間歇泉的地位是無庸置疑的。作為世界上最高的活躍間歇泉和地熱田，搭各加在海拔約五千一百米的高處也散發著自己熱氣騰騰的魅力。

這片地熱田不僅僅只有一群溫泉池，它還涵蓋了亞洲動力最大的間歇泉群。與之相鄰的是正在咕咕冒泡的地熱泉，總數超過百個，橫跨一公里長的廣闊地帶。這些地熱泉中，有大約二十個是真正的間歇泉，它們會週期性地爆發，噴出水和蒸氣，然後進入一段沉寂期。在西藏蒼茫的高原上，這些間歇泉猶如「忠誠而古老朋友」，與遙遠的美國西部黃石國家公園裡的地熱奇觀遙相呼應。它們當中最宏偉的成員，每三小時便要從深沉的夢鄉震撼地甦醒。而它的同伴們則更為靈動，或許十分鐘便上演一次噴薄而出的短促獨奏，接著又沉入長達一日以上的香甜睡眠。當這些熱泉迸發時，水柱肆無忌憚地直衝雲霄，高度可達驚人的七八米。這種由大自然親自操刀的夢幻秀實在迷人，更何況它不收門票，隨時歡迎人們光臨。

我長久地站在那座最大的噴泉旁。它不時地振奮精神，如同地底的巨龍，嘶吼著將滾燙的泉水噴向天際。熱騰騰的水蒸氣與西藏高原的冷空氣結合碰撞，翩翩起舞，變成淡淡的雲霧。然後它最多休息十分鐘，便會重複剛才的震撼表演，將水柱豪邁地射向二十米的高空，宛如一根寬達兩米的水矛，勇猛地刺破雲層。每一次的噴發，它周圍的地上都會留下一層又一層的鈣鹽寶石，彷彿是它千年時光的見證。

此刻，我不免回想起二〇〇二年，我在繞行岡仁波齊之後首次來到搭各加溫泉，時光荏苒，二十餘年轉瞬即逝。這一次，在我們從西藏西部前往新疆的途中，我終於有幸再次踏足這塊神奇的土地。我們在一個規模較小的溫泉邊安營紮寨，當地藏民以巧思導入近旁河流的清涼之水，把那蒸騰的湯池調和到了最適宜泡澡的溫度。在這個據說擁有療愈靈效的溫泉中沐浴過後，我們去拜訪了隔壁大帳篷裡的「鄰居」。

四十二歲的措仁・澤旺於今年四月來到此地，在帳篷中開設了一家既是雜貨鋪又是餐館的小店，主要服務那些慕名從遠處藏區來的藏民。每月他只能賺到微薄的兩千元人民幣，但他看起來樂在其中。措仁向我們透露，搭各加隱藏著一百零八處溫泉，每一處泉水都蘊藏著其獨特的神奇藥效，有的滋養肝臟，有的舒緩風濕，有的強健心脈，還有的神奇得如同萬能靈藥。其中一處溫泉更被傳說是昔日英雄格薩爾王的第一位王后布姆進行梳洗的神聖之地。

因著疫情的關係，在這幾年間，前往此處的遊客數量急劇減少。

A minor geyser / 相對較小的噴泉
Migrating Tibetan Antelope / 母藏羚羊遷徙

Tibetan bathers / 藏族沐浴者
Egg bathers boiled in pool / 在溫泉池煮蛋

然而最近似乎有漸漸回升的跡象。藏族牧民們會在七、八月間來此流連，而冬季時，許多人會來此紮營沐浴，一待就是半個月甚至更久。他們大多來自日喀則地區的薩迦縣和昂仁縣，以及阿里地區的措勤縣。從今年四月起，每天可能有十到二十名遊客來到這裡，雖然很少有人會留宿過夜。

我們經過這裡的原因，是為了趕往北方的改則縣。在這裡有一片廣袤無垠的羌塘國家級自然保護區，這是中國最大的自然保護區，多種藏區野生動物在此自由馳騁，其中包括野犛牛、藏羚羊、藏野驢、藏原羚、棕熊等眾多珍稀物種。

羌塘國家級自然保護區覆蓋了三十三萬四千平方公里的土地，什麼概念呢，就是這一個保護區的面積都快跟德國、芬蘭或馬來西亞整個國家差不多大了。整個區域的海拔高於四千五百米，部分地區甚至超過五千米。這裡有一條新公路，國道 216 號線，剛剛通車，穿越崇山峻嶺的西羌塘高原和東部的喀喇崑崙山脈，一直延伸到新疆的塔克拉瑪干沙漠盆地。我的計畫是在自駕遊客們湧入之前，悠閒地穿越這八百多公里的荒野，但顯然，萬事不由人。

露營過夜後，我們一大早就抵達了改則。行經這條新鋪設的道路需要獲得特別的通行許可，包括攜帶灌滿油的備用油罐也要經過許可，這可是必需品，因為在西藏到新疆之間沒有加油站。政府辦公室上午九點開門，我們趕到時，前面已經是大排長龍的狀態了，我們的三輛車拿到了二十七到二十九號。意想不到的是，剛剛好，我們後面再沒人拿到號碼牌了，因為辦公室中午十二點就要關門，下午也不再開放。牆上貼著一張告示，新路從明天起因大範圍驗收檢查將再次封閉。我們成為了最後一批被放行的車輛，要求是每個人必須在午夜前，通過超過四百公里西藏這邊的公路。

在政府辦公室門前，一隊載著嶄新油罐的皮卡車彷彿一群勤勞的小蜜蜂。我們迅速買下四罐珍貴的「能量黃金」，為我們的鋼鐵駿馬裝填彈藥。在辦公室即將關閉的最後一刻，我們手捧著通行證，像是終於等到了一道聖旨。飛奔至最近的加油站，讓座駕喝飽，我們也顧不上自己飢腸轆轆的肚子，匆匆忙忙地就上路了。與即將封閉的道路賽跑，爭分奪秒，好像是電子遊戲裡才有的刺激場面，就這麼在我們身上真實上演了。

新鋪設的路面平坦易行，卻也是一張西藏高原極具誘惑力的邀請函，它低語著讓我們放慢腳步，與大自然肩並肩。但是我們可是身後有截至時限追著的人啊！於是每個人的內心都戲劇性地上演著一場拉鋸戰，一邊是對捕捉身旁美景的渴望，一邊則是對紀律的尊重堅守。然而，大自然的召喚總是能以壓倒性的勝利結束辯論，理智思維對自律的呼喚都被輕柔的風吹散。

六月的陽光下，雌性藏羚羊如同季節的鐘擺，準時向著山中神祕的繁殖地移動。當偶遇這些高原的舞者時，我們情不自禁地按下了停息的按鈕，讓無人機成為我們的眼睛，隨牠們在草原上起舞。比較令人驚喜的是，這些群居的精靈們對於頭頂的機械鳥翼絲毫不為所動，依然自在地漫步、覓食。我想，這也算是對過去三十年保護工作的良好交代。

然而，遇到野驢時就是另一番景象，牠們一旦察覺到我們靠近，就會迅速集結，立即朝反方向跑去，

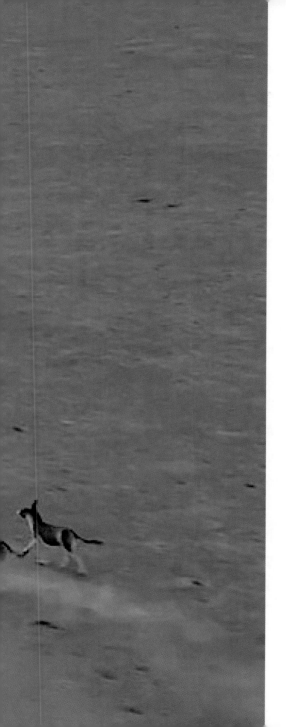

有時無人機的接近甚至會引發牠們的驚慌奔逃。途中我們只偶遇過一次野犛牛，因為時間緊迫，只能遠遠地捕捉幾張照片。道路兩旁，積雪的山峰圍繞著原始的湖泊，宛如潔淨的仙境，穿過其中不久，我們進入到了一個彷彿被火焰親吻過的地區，兩旁的焦黑巖石像是經歷過洪荒之火的證人，靜默地守護著這片土地，而在它們的身後，是那些被白雪加冕的巍峨山脈。在這樣令人敬畏的高度，雨水很快會變成冰雹，再化成雪花，如同變幻莫測的魔法。每一片雪花都像是對我們即將進入乾燥炎熱沙漠的最後祝福，一場天空的狂歡，在我們下撤前的一剎那，熱情地舞動。

終於，隨著我們穿越那座高聳的山口，眼前展開了一片銀裝素裹的世界。就在路邊，一塊標誌牌靜默地告訴我們已經進入了神祕的新疆。這個地方值得我們停下腳步，來一張合影留念。而不久後我們將踏上的這片土地，正是被西方媒體描畫為「集中營」的那片區域。這種

Wild Ass stampeding / 奔逃的野驢

充滿偏見，不顧事實，完全喪失邏輯的報導，正讓西方媒體逐漸失去他們的一些包括我在內的老朋友。畢竟朋友之間靠的是信任，是對彼此優良品質的惺惺相惜。好在自一九七九年起，我在不斷地來回新疆的過程中，結交了許多當地的朋友。

我總是說，話語是多餘且廉價的。看看一個孩子或者老人的眼睛，那才能告訴你更多的故事。不幸的是，在這個年代，虛假的東西似乎比真情實感傳播得更快更廣，因為大眾總是對戲劇性的故事垂涎三尺。每個國家的媒體都要為其政治需求服務，不同的只是包裝的高明程度。做得好時，我們稱之有「新聞自由」；不好時，就被斥為政治宣傳。此刻，我有些為自己沉醉在大自然賜予的絕美景色中時，還能想到一些垃圾一樣的政治表達而神傷。

面對這條品質優良的公路，我不禁好奇，他們為何還要閉路檢查。是不是出於軍事後勤的考慮呢？如果是，也無可厚非。對於任何國家來說，這都是理所當然的事。夜幕尚未降臨，我們已深入新疆腹地，只見藏羚羊從西邊的山坡往上緩緩遷徙。此時大約是晚上九點，天空依然明亮，畢竟新疆距離北京有三個時區，但卻遵照著首都的全國標準時間。行至夜色漸濃時，那長長的下坡路跑起來依然美不勝收。距離塔克拉瑪干沙漠南緣的民豐小鎮，還有大約三百公里的路程。

新疆有句古老的諺語，在我從高原下降至世界第二大流動沙漠的深處時，似乎更顯得貼切：「早穿棉襖午穿紗，抱著火爐吃西瓜。」這是對幾小時內戲劇性氣候變化的生動描述。作為一名探險者，我已經習慣了擁抱這些極端。從西藏進入新疆，正是這種極端的美好體現。

Road with snow / 積雪的道路
Team CERS into Xinjiang / 探險學會進疆紀念

從西藏到新疆（下）

TIBET BY A NEW ROAD INTO XINJIANG (Part 2)

Dunhuang – June 23, 2023

TIBET BY A NEW ROAD INTO XINJIANG (Part 2)

From Minfeng in Xinjiang westward to Yutian is around 110 kilometers and takes barely over an hour to drive. I decide to go there for a quick revisit, having been there multiple times since 1984. CERS has a small collection of ethnic hats from China, and the Uighur women of Yutian (Keriya in old days) claim to wear the smallest hat in the world. It has an embroidered silk top with a bottom woven from black sheep wool, measuring a tiny ten centimeters in diameter at the base. Usually it is worn on top of a married lady's head veil. We are successful in getting one fine specimen, including a full costume, directly from a museum. It will grace our collection of artifacts inside the newly constructed Xinjiang Pavilion at our Center in Shangri-la.

Little remains of the traditional old town of Yutian. We have lunch at a posh and popular Uighur restaurant where the naan bread is freshly baked in a mud oven outside and the mutton on metal sticks is also cooked over an open grill. Nearby are many fruit stands where we treat ourselves to some wonderful peaches, apricots, melon and, surprisingly, local mangoes just in season. Unfortunately, the famous Xinjiang grapes are still out of season. But wines made from those same grapes are now available in many shops.

Today some of the old markets have been replaced by huge food court halls with all types of eatery

Section of Old Town Yutian / 于闐的舊城區   Old Town Fruit Stand / 舊城區的水果攤

booths. The one we visit comes with organized song and dance performances by local neighborhood troupes who volunteer to go on stage to entertain the diners. Their enthusiasm and joy hardly match what we read in outside media with its reports of an oppressed people. Other accounts around the world are largely through syndication of these branded media with little means of fact checking. Any country would have plenty of people with grievances, true as they may be. But for political reasons, the media would choose to report only on the negative, even if mostly exceptions rather than the norm.

Yutian is also where, in 1993, we began a small-scale excavation at Lao Damagou near the ancient ruin of Niya. Niya had been visited and excavated by several early explorers from the West, and it was thus made famous in their writings. Together with Mr. Li Yinping, director of the Hotan (Khotan) Institute of Archaeology, we used the latest metal detector brought from the US to find some old coins, besides recovery of some early ceramic shards.

Restaurant in Yutian / 于闐的餐廳

This project led to another in 1994. With support from Dr Charles Elachi, Director of the Jet Propulsion Laboratory in Pasadena California, we used the new Space Shuttle Imaging Radar (SIR-C) to scan the earth, looking for important additional sites inside the desert of Qiemo, some four hundred kilometers to the east of Yutian.

One of the properties of the radar is that it could penetrate underground in extremely dry desert areas to a depth of three meters or more. My current philosophy is that archaeological sites and relics are better kept underground than bringing them to the surface, where huge resources may be needed to keep and maintain them. The radar data, however, can be crucial for future archaeological discoveries and protection, not to mention for survey of subsurface aqua reservoirs.

We do travel to Qiemo before taking leave of Xinjiang. A sandstorm hits Qiemo while we are there, and overnight our cars are covered with a layer of fine sand. We decide to retreat into the mountains, the foothills of the Kunlun which is an extension of the Karakoram. There, at the village of Kulamulake some ninety kilometers from Qiemo we are hidden among mountains and shielded from the storm far below. The new village, with some five hundred inhabitants, is just in the process of turning their old home higher up the mountain into a tourist site. It is intended for locals to

Naan bread baker / 烤饢的師父
Fruit drink at food hall / 美食廣場的果汁

escape the summer heat of the desert to enjoy the cool mountain air.

I stay in my camper van for the night while some in my team take to homestay inside a large yurt. Next to us are two half-buried underground houses, dug out to avoid the summer heat and winter cold. A small exhibit had been set up inside to display many objects formerly used by the Uighur villagers. There are utensils and artifacts made from desert poplar tree, a resilient plant that can survive the most extreme climate for a thousand years. There are also other functional items made from leather with Uighur motifs.

At one traditional village home, we visit an elderly Uighur couple. Bijang is 75 years old and his wife Guli is 73. The new village of Kulamulake has a hundred and fifty households with 553 villagers. Originally these people all lived in this ancient village, now called Kunlun Old Village, but everyone has moved to the new settlement in 2016. Now the villagers have come back to try to

Bijang & Guli / 比江和古麗　　　　　　Happy dancing picnic / 快樂歌舞野餐

develop the old site into a new attraction. As for the elderly couple, they could not get used to staying at the newly constructed village and decided to move back for good. With ten mou of private land, they grow crops like millet, barley and garlic, which provides subsistence for themselves. They also have twenty sheep and one camel, one cow and some forty pigeon that they raise.

Bijang and Guli have six grown children. Five of them are girls and all married long ago. Their son has established his own family with two daughters and has decided to live in the new village. He has a total of over 150 sheep. One grandkid is now attending university at Urumqi studying design art. Each year around mid April, the family all come together at the old village to help the old couple in ploughing to start a new season of farming. In September, there will be another round of reunion during harvest time when more hands are needed in the field. Other festive times, like Ramadan and Eid al-Adha, the family would of course also get together.

Only about ten to twenty villagers still live permanently in the Kunlun Old Village. There is no mosque, thus no gathering for prayers. Fewer and fewer people dress in traditional costume on a daily basis. Younger Uighur have all opted for modernized dress, except perhaps during wedding or festival time. At time of our visit, several families are there having a dancing picnic.

When the desert storm subsides the following day, we move back into Qiemo and visited a very special archaeological site at the edge of the desert. Zagunluke was first discovered in 1930 - a group of five burial sites in an area spreading over some two kilometers. Since the pandemic, few visitors come out to the edge of the desert. We manage to find the gate-keeper who allows us into the small exhibit museum.

There constructed in situ is one of the oldest tombs with human remains including adults and infants. The tallest man measured over 1.8 meters. These remains are said to be from around 3000 years ago. Many of the displayed corpses still look vivid, with the original facial features and their hair still intact, thanks to the dry desert that helped in preserving them.

After a brief visit to the museum, we venture to drive out into the desert for about one kilometer in order to check out another excavation site, the ruins of an ancient settlement along the Silk Road. But less than a hundred meters off-road into the desert, the camper van is hopelessly mired and stuck in the fine sand. Multiple efforts only spin the wheels and sink the van further. We are not successful in freeing it and I decide to use the power winch of the Land Rover to extract the sad vehicle. With some digging and pushing on the side, inch by inch we manage to gradually get the camper back on solid ground. We leave the camper by the road and explore the distant site using our two Land Rovers by engaging our four-wheel drive. This last episode of getting stuck in the desert reminds me of the countless times of such ordeals in my earlier years of exploring into the desert after the 1980s.

From Qiemo we drive east entering Ruoqiang, the largest county of China with an area of over 200,000 square kilometers, almost the same size as Korea. It encompasses the huge 45,000-square-kilometer Altun Mountain Nature Reserve, at one time the largest inland nature reserve in the world. This is where CERS studied wildlife for many years, especially when I served as the reserve's Chief Advisor in the 1990s.

We have now driven over 10,000 kilometers and there is an urge to take a rest. Crossing into Qinghai, we drive north and reach the oasis city of Dunhuang in Gansu Province. The posh Dunhuang Silk Road Hotel lays out the red carpet to receive us. CERS maintained a center of operations for northwest China here in the 1990s. We are led into the most exclusive courtyard suite with four rooms. This is where Bill Gates once stayed when he visited Dunhuang around 1996.

After giving ourselves a thorough cleaning up to shed off the dust of the desert, we shall take a three to four days well deserved hiatus, before making our final leg and the long drive back to our Zhongdian Center in Yunnan. Short and limited my observations in Xinjiang may be, I certainly feel more qualified to reflect on the area, than from those who hasn't been there lately or at all, yet feel free to make allegations and judgement about this faraway place.

Burial site museum / 墓葬遺跡展覽館
Burial display / 展覽館裡的墓地

從西藏到新疆（下）煥然一新的老朋友

從新疆的民豐至西端的于闐，路程大約一百一十公里，一個多小時的車程便可抵達。自一九八四年起，我已數次踏足這片土地，這次我決定故地重遊，追尋那些熟悉的回憶。中國探險學會收藏了少量來自中國少數民族的帽子，于闐，舊稱克里雅的特色小帽自然勾起了我們的興趣。據當地的維吾爾族女性說，這是世界上最小的帽子。這種帽子上部繡有絲綢，下部以黑羊毛編織，底徑僅有微小的十公分，已婚女性通常將其戴在珠飾面紗之上。我們有幸從一家博物館直接獲得了一整套珍貴的當地民族服裝，準備帶回學會香格里拉中心新建的新疆館用於展覽。

于闐的老城巷弄已然所剩不多，但依舊充滿魅力。我們在一家很火爆的維吾爾高檔餐廳用餐，那裡的饢餅熱騰騰，剛從屋外的泥爐中取出，鐵棍上羊肉在露天烤架上滋滋冒著熱氣。附近的水果攤擺滿了當季的蜜桃、杏子和甜瓜，意外的是當地的芒果也適逢產季，黃燦燦的很誘人。不過有點遺憾的是，著名的新疆葡萄這個時節還未成熟，還好那些葡萄釀造的葡萄酒在許多商店都能買到。

如今，一些舊市場已被巨大的美食廣場所取代，裡面林立著形形色色的小吃攤。我們吃飯的這個地方，甚至還有當地街坊組成的表演團自發登台唱歌跳舞，為用餐的顧客活躍氣氛。他們的熱情與歡樂，與一些媒體描繪的受壓迫的民眾形象大相逕庭。某些知名度較高的媒體大肆宣揚一些未經核實的消息，導致前段時間全球性的輿論爆發。任何國家都做不到讓它的每一個民眾都毫無怨言，這點確實無法否認。但出於政治原因，只帶選擇性誇大報導個例而非常態的負面消息，這種做法就太令人失望了。

一九九三年，我們還曾在于闐進行過一場小規模的挖掘活動，地點位於尼雅古城遺址附近的老達馬溝。早期的西方探險家曾對尼雅古城進行過挖掘，相關著作也頗具盛名。當時我們是與和田考古研究所所長李吟平先生一起，用的是從美國帶來的最新款金屬探測器，在尋獲了一些早期陶瓷碎片之外，還發現了一些古老的硬幣。這個項目在一九九四年還有後續。在加州帕薩迪納美國航天署的噴氣推進實驗室 *(JPL)* 主任查爾斯・埃拉奇博士的支持下，我們得以使用當時最新型的太空梭成像雷達（*SIR-C*）來掃描地面，尋找位於且末沙漠內部，距離于闐東方約四百公里的重要新遺址。

這種雷達的特性之一，是能夠在極度乾燥的沙漠地區穿透地下三米甚至更深的土層。我目前的觀點是，遺址和文物留在地下比挖掘出來更好，因為一旦挖掘出地面，可能需要巨大的資源來保護和維護它們，而這有時會超出我們現在的能力範圍。當然，雷達技術是頂好的，因為它能收集到的資料對未來的考古發現和保護至關重要，更別說是調查地下水源了。

Uyghur lady with tiny hat /
戴著小帽子的維吾爾族女士
Night market performance / 夜市表演

冥冥之中，在我們離開新疆之前，我又回了一趟且末沙漠。正值我們在當地，一場的沙塵暴不期而至，一夜之間我們的車都被細沙覆蓋。此刻，撤退是個好主意，我們於是退入崑崙山的懷抱，那裡是喀喇崑崙山脈的延續，在離且末九十公里的庫拉木拉克村，讓群山為我們擋風遮沙。這個寧靜而安詳的新興小村莊，擁有約五百名居民，他們正在努力將山上的老屋子變為景區，讓當地居民們也可以逃離沙漠的熾熱，享受山間的清涼。

那一晚，我選擇在我的露營車內安眠，而我的隊友們則在一頂寬敞的氈房內借宿，看著倒也不失溫馨。旁邊，兩座半埋入地面的房屋靜靜躺在那裡，巧妙的特殊構造是為了逃避夏日的炎熱與冬日的寒冷。其中一間布置了一個小型展覽，展出了維吾爾村民曾用的各式物件。所有這些用品和工藝品都出自堅韌非常的沙漠楊樹，這種植物能在極端惡劣的氣候中存活千年。還有一些皮革製品，上面繡有精美的維吾爾族圖騰。

我們還拜訪了一對維吾爾族老夫婦，比江今年七十五歲，他的妻子古麗七十三歲。庫拉木拉克新村里有一百五十戶人家，共五百五十三名村民。這些人原本居住在現名為崑崙老村的古村，但二〇一六年全村搬遷至新址。現在村民們又都短暫地回到了老村，

Artifacts on display / 展出的手工藝品

Underground abode / 地下的居所

Traditional home / 傳統民居

希望將這裡建設成旅遊景點。至於那對老夫婦，他們適應不了新村莊的生活，於是決定永遠搬回老村。他們在這裡有十畝土地，平日種小米、大麥和大蒜，除此之外，還養著二十隻羊、一隻駱駝、一頭牛和大約四十隻鴿子，所以不僅是能做到基本的自給自足，老倆口的田園生活也稱得上豐富。

比江和古麗育有六個孩子，其中五個是閨女，早已出嫁。他們的獨子在新村落建立了自己的小家庭並打算長居此地，他家育有兩個可愛的女兒，還有超過一百五十隻羊，可謂是羊群小霸王。家族中有個小孫子目前正在烏魯木齊的大學研習設計藝術，是全家人的小驕傲。每年四月中旬，一家人都會齊聚老村，幫老倆口開始新一季的耕作。九月收穫季節則又是一個家族團聚的好時機，因為此時田裡總需要幫手。在其他節慶日，如齋戒月和古爾邦節，家族自然也會歡聚一堂。

如今，崑崙老村僅有約十到二十個村民常住。由於沒有清真寺，所以也沒有日常的禱告活動。傳統服飾的穿戴者日益稀少，年輕的維吾爾族人都偏好現代化的衣著，只有在婚禮或節日之時才會換上傳統盛裝。在我們造訪的時候，有幾家人正在那兒享受著悠閒的野餐時光，大家在燒烤爐旁載歌載舞，好不熱鬧。

經過一夜沙塵暴的洗禮，天色剛一放晴，我們便重返且末，踏向沙漠邊緣的一處神祕遺址——扎滾魯克。這片寶地於一九三〇年首次揭開其神祕面紗，現包括五個散布在兩公里方圓內的古墓。自疫情以來，這裡鮮少有遊客踏足。幸運的我們找到了守護這片古蹟的看門人，他引我們進入了一座規模雖小但內容豐厚的展覽館。

重建於原址之上的，是一座藏有成人及嬰兒遺骸的古老墓穴。其中一位男性遺骸長達一米八以上。這些沉睡的靈魂據說已有三千年歷史，在乾燥沙漠氣候的悉心保護下，這些古人的面容和髮絲竟仍然栩栩如生。

博物館之後，我們決心驅車深入沙漠一公里，探索另一處絲綢之路沿線的古代民居。然而，剛離開鋪好的道路不足百米，我們的露營車便被細沙無情吞噬，再三努力卻只是徒增困境。無奈之下，只能依靠我們路虎越野車的力量，加上人力在旁邊又拉又推，用絞盤一寸寸地將這可憐的四輪戰士拯救出沙海。留下露營車守衛道旁，我們駕駛兩輛四驅路虎，繼續向那遙遠的遺址進發。這次困境，勾起了我對八〇年代以來無數次艱難但刺激的沙漠探險的回憶。

從且末出發，我們向東進入若羌縣，這是一片跟整個韓國國土面積差不多大的廣袤土地，占地面積超過二十萬平方公里。這裡還擁有四萬五千平方公里的阿爾金山自然保護區，曾是全球最大的內陸自然保護區。九〇年代，正是在這片廣闊的土地上，我曾作為保護區首席顧問，與 CERS 一起進行了多年的野生動物研究工作。

行駛逾萬公里後，大家都已經疲憊不堪了。穿越青海，向北直行，我們終於抵達甘肅省那片令人心曠神怡的綠洲城市，敦煌。這裡的敦煌山莊酒店熱情似火，紅地毯在門口滾滾鋪開，讓人想感受不到熱情都難。回想上世紀九〇年代，CERS 還曾在這裡設立中國西北項目中心。我們入住的是一間典雅非凡的四合院庭院套間，講個趣事，這兒正是比爾·蓋茨一九九六年訪問敦煌時住的地方。

在澈底洗去一身塵土後，我們將在這裡享受三到四天的寧靜閒暇，之後再經歷一段漫長的車程返回雲南的中甸中心。儘管我對新疆的觀察可能短暫也有些粗略，但相對於那些近期甚至從未親臨其境，卻對這遙遠之地妄加評論的人，我覺得我更有話語權。嘴長在別人身上我們也管不了，但是我還是強烈建議大家靠自己身體，真實地去體驗這個世界。

Happy Desert Camping / 愉快的沙漠露營

絲
路
沿
線
的
黃
金
寶
塔

GOLDEN PAGODA ALONG THE SILK ROAD

Jinta, Gansu – June 25, 2023

GOLDEN PAGODA ALONG THE SILK ROAD

Faqi was head administering monk at Nanhua Monastery, senior deputy to the abbot of that ancient temple in northern Guangdong. It was where the famous Tang Dynasty 6th Patriarch Master Huineng, a Zen monk, lived in the 7th century. I visited the monastery in 2015, introduced by the venerable monk Xingyun of Taiwan and stayed there overnight as Chinese New Year's Eve crossed into the first morning of the next year.

I was warmly received by Faqi, as he had studied under Xingyun while in Taiwan. I was taught not only a lesson about Patriarch Master Huineng, but also a game of ping pong by Kung Fu Faqi as he was a former champion at his hometown in Gansu. I had a short visit with the chief abbot as well, and I noted in my writing that it was a rather cordial audience and mentioned the many valuable gifts inside his home. I further commented that such items would be much appreciated if put on public display inside the monastery for everyone to see.

But it was not to be, as in 2021, Faqi finally was forced to write an exposé on the internet, describing the many irregularities at the monastery and discrediting the various deeds of his head abbot. It included accusations of the privatizing of many of the monastery's holdings by putting them with his relatives who were operating several profit-making and privileged sectors of the monastery, as well as the construction of illegal and unsafe structure within the compound without acquiring permission from the building ordinance office.

The disputes escalated into mudslinging with counter accusations, to an extent that Faqi was sent to a sanitorium as if having gone crazy. It then descended into his being driven out of the monastery. As with many cases where local government is drawn in, certain bureaucrats came out front to take sides, in this case in defense of the abbot. Ultimately, investigation of such matters often reveals conflict of interest among the parties involved, though this particular case was never openly resolved in public view. I, as well as others, can draw their own conclusions. As the Chinese saying goes, "wind doesn't blow from inside an empty cave."

Like Huineng, who was chased away from Shaolin Monastery before winding up in the southern province, Faqi was persecuted, ostracized and driven away, ending up in the distant northwest. It was with such matters hanging over my mind that I contacted Faqi, who had gone home to Jiayuguan in Gansu along the Old Silk Road. Despite my worries, he had fared well. He had quickly ended up associated with another ancient Buddhist site, Jinta Temple, unlike the Patriarch Huineng himself, who had hidden in the remotest parts of Guangdong, living among forest hunters for

Nanhua Monastery / 南華寺
Main Hall Nanhua Monastery / 南華寺大殿

sixteen years before resurfacing at Nanhua Monastery.

Thus it was that I found Faqi here in Jiayuguan after some search, and he led me to Jinta to spend two days there. Like Nanhua Monastery, Jinta Temple hailed also from the Tang Dynasty, and possibly earlier. Some accounts had it being founded during the Eastern Jin or Northern Wei dynasties of the 4th Century, close to 1700 years ago. Jinta Temple (meaning Golden Pagoda in Chinese) is in Jinta County, Jiuquan City of Gansu Province. Jinta is the only county in China named after a Buddhist temple. It is located in the Gansu corridor on the Silk Road, at a far western point that all ancient traders, pilgrims and government officials had to pass through on their way to the western frontiers. It is quite possible that Buddhist masters like Faxian of the Eastern Jin Dynasty and Xuanzang of the Tang Dynasty passed through here, stopping to pay homage to the Golden Pagoda before continuing on their journey to India in pursuit of the original Buddhist scriptures.

Jiayuguan, which is close to Jinta Temple, was a military outpost and fortress at the western end of the Great Wall, famous at home and abroad. The Golden Pagoda, however, is a sacred site of worship that holds its own significance in the region. Though not comparable to many of today's tourist attraction religious sites with extravagant monastic architecture, the golden pagoda's existence has conformed to the highest canon of Buddhism in history. It is a perfect example of what an original temple should be - a simple and dignified religious place of worship that enhances the spiritual pursuit and purity of the mind. The Jinta Temple preserves well the exquisite essence of the ancient monasteries and provides a place full of peace and tranquility.

Jinta Pagoda / 金塔

The reconstruction and restoration of Jinta Temple over centuries consolidated its history up to the modern age. By the end of the Ming dynasty, the pagoda had collapsed once, but its foundation remained. In 1700, the Qing Kangxi Emperor rebuilt the copper top structure, recording that the pagoda was seven feet in circumference and five feet in height, and the top was five feet in additional height and about one foot to two feet in circumference. The whole reconstruction took three years to complete. In 1732, a monk disciple by the name of Muhua renovated the front and back pavilions and added the drum and bell towers.

During restoration in 1987, four wooden tablets were rediscovered at the top of the pagoda. They recorded four previous periods of repair to the big pagoda, in 1707, 1778, 1845 and 1923 respectively. In both 1987 and 2011, during the last two rounds of restoration of the big pagoda, additional relics and sutras were uncovered, dating from the Ming and Qing dynasties. Among many Class 3 artifacts of China's national treasures were some assigned to Class 1 and 2. These included some early scriptures written in the Ming and Qing dynasties, which are now in the Jinta County Museum.

On the architectural side, the Jinta Temple restoration assiduously retained traditional construction methods and styles from China's Western regions and Central Asia. For example, during the maintenance in the 1980s, the Ming dynasty architectural method was applied to restore the old pagoda, and the mud processing techniques used were ancient. The triad soil was mixed with glutinous rice porridge and cotton to increase the viscosity and strength of the mix, so as to prevent cracking once dried. The dried walls were smeared twice with pig's blood, and then the entire tower was painted with red clay and sprayed with a protective agent to restore the old appearance of the golden tower.

There are many Buddhist pagodas in China and neighboring Asian countries, but the Jinta Temple is a special case of a pagoda being the basis of a temple. Located along the ancient Silk Road, it has witnessed thousands of years of history and cultural exchanges between Chinese and Western religious traditions, from ancient through modern times until today.

Faqi & Longzheng at meal / 法啟與龍正在吃飯

I befriended the 42-years-old caretaker monk Longzheng at Jinta Temple. He too is from Jiayuguan. At the age of 12 in 1993 while he was attending primary three, he got attracted to Buddhism and began visiting Jinta Temple, and he soon entered monkhood. Though he had to stay in school, he spent all his spare time studying Buddhism and conducted all necessary religious exercises and discipline.

At the time he turned 18, Longzheng went to Lanzhou the provincial capital and studied Buddhism at the Junyuan Monastery, becoming a full-time monk and severing all connection to his family and home. This was followed by more study in Hunan under three famous masters. Then, in 2005, at an age of 26, Longzheng went to Wutai Shan, the famous pilgrim

Inside Temple / 寺內景觀

mountain in Shanxi Province. In 2007, answering the call of his first master teacher, he returned to Jinta and there entered into long meditation for the next 16 years. It was only four months before my visit that Longzheng exited meditation and took up a position as head monk and caretaker of Jinta Temple.

At present, Jinta only has a total of four resident monks; Longzheng, my friend Faqi as disciplinary monk, and two junior monks, Duli and Duqing. When Longzheng first returned in 2007, there were seven monks, but three senior monks have passed away one after another. Whenever there are chanting events, supplicants from nearby towns and countryside would participate and fill in. Daily chores and cleaning duties are performed by some twenty or so Buddhist followers in the vicinity.

Longzheng became my good friend, just like Faqi, who was very happy that we got reunited. My two short days at Jinta were both pleasant and tranquil, certainly beating the pomp and circumstance of many of the overly posh and glittering temples and monasteries that I have visited in the past. Before I left, Longzheng and the other monks asked me earnestly whether I could help them write up a description of Jinta for printing. I gladly obliged and promised that they would soon receive text and photos to use for printing a flyer or leaflet, glorifying the history and simplicity of this little-known yet important temple along the old Silk Road.

As with Nanhua Monastery in Guangdong from which Faqi was evicted, the spirit of Huineng, the Sixth Patriarch Monk, would surely do his duty and return the dignity of this site to its rightful place. Hopefully sooner rather than later.

絲路沿線的黃金寶塔

在廣東北部，南華寺的影壁之下，法啟曾擔任行政副住持的重任。這座歷史悠久的殿堂，曾是唐代禪宗六祖慧能大師在西元七世紀的靜修之地。二〇一五年，在我尊敬的台灣星雲大師的引薦下，我踏入了這片靈山聖地，並有幸於中國新年之際在此留宿，迎接新年的第一縷晨光。

彼時，法啟熱誠地迎接了我，這分溫暖源於他曾在台灣隨星雲大師學道的緣分。在那次深度交談中，我不僅深入了解了六祖慧能大師的禪學思想，還與曾獲甘肅地區乒乓球冠軍的「功夫大師」法啟切磋了球技。此外，我還短暫地拜會了住持，我的筆記中記載下了許多他家中的珍貴寶物。我曾建議，若能將這些珍品於寺院中公諸於世，它們必定能受到更多的珍視與讚譽。

但世事發展總是讓人難以預料。二〇二一年時，法啟終於忍無可忍地在網絡上發表了一篇揭露性的文章，揭開了寺院中眾多不合規之事，並指控其住持行為不端。文章中詳述了一系列問題，包括住持將寺院資產私有化，轉移給經營數個盈利及特權部門的親屬，以及在未獲得正式許可的情況下，非法建造不安全的建築。這種種一切，都將古寺背後的波濤暗湧推到了臺前。

紛爭如野火般迅速蔓延，演變成一場激烈的互相指控，法啟不可避免地被風暴吞噬，一度要被當作瘋子送進療養院。直到他被迫離開了寺院，事態才稍微平息。如同大多涉及地方政府的案子，某些官僚人員總會在最後出面選邊站，這一次，他們站在了住持那一邊。這類看似充滿迷霧的案子，往往最能揭示參與各方之間錯綜複雜的利益糾葛。儘管此案從未在陽光下清晰呈現，我與其他旁觀者還是能根據這片混沌自行拼湊出一些真相。老話總是蘊含最直白的道理：「無風不起浪，空穴不來風。」

就像被少林寺驅逐，然後輾轉流浪南方各省的禪宗六祖慧能，法啟也一路遭到迫害、排斥，最後落腳在偏遠的西北。我心裡一直掛念著這些事，於是聯繫了返回甘肅嘉峪關的法啟。此時我心中還充滿憂慮，生怕他像當年的慧能一樣隱居起來，在廣東最偏僻的森林中，與獵人共處長達十六年，才重新面世。還好我的擔心是多餘的，法啟似乎在新的環境中找到了屬於自己的安寧。他很快便與另一座充滿歷史氣息的佛教聖地金塔寺結下了不解之緣。

因此，在經過一番尋覓後，我在嘉峪關找到了法啟，他引我前往金塔寺，在那裡度過了兩天。如同南華寺一樣，金塔寺自唐代以來便盛名遠播，甚至可能更早於此。有文獻記載，其創建於東晉或北魏時期，大約在公元四世紀，距今已近一千七百年。金塔寺位於甘肅省酒泉市金塔縣，這是中國唯一以佛教寺廟命名的縣。

Faqi & HM / 法啟與 HM
HM with Faqi & Longzheng / HM 與法啟和龍正

Pagoda & temple / 金塔與廟
Jinta Temple / 金塔寺
Jiayuguan circa 1979 / 1979 年前後的嘉峪關

它座落於絲綢之路上的河西走廊，這個極西點是所有古代商人、朝聖者及官員前往西部邊疆的必經之地。東晉的法顯和唐代的玄奘等佛教大師，很可能都曾經過此地，在繼續前往印度尋求佛教經典前，向此地的金塔頂禮膜拜，祈求平安。

鄰近金塔寺的嘉峪關，是萬里長城最西端的軍事前哨和要塞，在國內外都很有名。不過金塔寺也很有名，它本身是一個具有重要地區意義的朝聖地。雖然它的規模無法與今日許多擁有奢華寺院建築的宗教觀光勝地相比，但其存在卻恪守佛教歷史上最高的經典準則。它有著一座原始寺廟該有的所有樣子，簡樸而威嚴，於我而言，反而比其他寺廟更能淨化心智，提升心靈追求。

數世紀的重建與修復，讓金塔寺的歷史一直延續到現代。明朝末年，塔身曾一度倒塌，但基座仍然存在。一七〇〇年，清康熙皇帝重建了銅制頂結構，當時的記錄顯示，重製的塔身周長七尺，高五尺，而塔頂額外高五尺，周長約一至二尺，整個重建工程耗時三年完成。一七三二年，一位名為木華的僧侶修繕了前後兩座亭子，並增設了鼓樓和鐘樓。

Pagoda Top / 金塔頂端
Pagoda base / 金塔底座

在一九八七年的修復過程中，人們於塔頂發現了四塊木牌。牌上是此前四次對大寶塔的修繕紀錄，年分顯示，四次修繕分別發生在一七〇七年、一七七八年、一八四五年和一九二三年。在一九八七年和二〇一一年最近的兩次大塔修復期間，還發現了許多來自明清時期的文物和經文。如今的中國國家三級保護文物中，其實有很多是從前被界定為一級和二級的，其中就包括這些明清時代的經文，現存於金塔縣博物館中。

在建築方面，金塔寺的修復工作始終堅持用來自中國西部地區及中亞的傳統建造方法和風格。尤其在八〇年代的修繕過程中，工匠們運用明代流傳下來的建築智慧，為古老的塔身注入了新生命，使用的泥土處理技術也同樣古老，但非常適用。修復中使用的三合土，融合了糯米粥和棉花，這種混合物不僅增強了黏性和堅韌度，更是對抗時間侵蝕的盾牌，能有效防止牆壁乾燥後的裂痕。當牆壁乾透後，工人們會分兩次將豬血抹上，隨後再覆上紅泥，噴灑保護劑。這一層層的塗抹，更像是一種古老儀式的再現，修復的過程就像慢慢把寶塔從時間的漩渦中拉出來一樣，再見面時，它帶著歷史的厚重，但仍掩不住嶄新的光芒。

金塔寺見證了千年來中西宗教傳統之間的文化交流。在中國和鄰近的亞洲國家中，佛教寶塔數不勝數，但金塔寺是以佛塔作為寺廟基礎的特例。

我在金塔寺結識了四十二歲的住持龍正，他也來自嘉峪關。一九九三年，當他十二歲上小學三年級時，就被佛教吸引，開始參訪金塔寺，不久後便出家為僧。儘管他必須繼續在學校學習，但他利用所有空閒時間學習佛法，並要求自己執行所有必要的宗教修行和紀律。

十八歲時，龍正前往甘肅省會蘭州，在浚源寺研習佛法，成為了一名全職僧侶，與家鄉斷絕了所有

Vegetarian meal / 素食

聯繫。此後，他在湖南跟隨三位著名的大師進一步學習。二〇〇五年，龍正二十六歲時前往山西省著名的朝聖地五臺山待了兩年。二〇〇七年，應其首位師父的召喚，他返回金塔，並在此開始了長達十六年的坐禪。就在我拜訪前四個月，龍正才剛出關，接任金塔寺住持的位置。

目前，金塔寺僅有四位常住僧侶：擔任戒律僧的法啟、我的新朋友龍正，以及兩位初學僧人都立和都清。二〇〇七年龍正剛返回金塔時，寺中共有七位僧人，但三位老僧先後辭世。於是每當舉行誦經活動人手不夠時，鄰近鎮上和鄉村的信眾都會過來幫忙。日常的雜務和清潔工作則由附近的約二十名佛教信徒負責。

這裡的生活，宛如一幅恬靜愉悅的水墨畫，沒有一絲我曾遊歷的許多奢華閃耀的寺廟和修道院所散發的浮華氣息。在我準備離開之際，龍正和其他僧人滿含誠意地請求我撰寫一篇關於金塔寺的文章，想要印在宣傳冊上，讓外界認識這座位於古絲綢之路要道上的隱祕之地，了解其悠久歷史與質樸風貌。我欣然接受了這一請求，並承諾不久後就會發來文字和照片。

一千多年前，六祖慧能用強大的精神振興了南華寺。一千多年後，法啟從那裡被驅逐，帶著慧能的精神來到了金塔。我相信法啟，能讓這金塔寺得到它應有的尊重和地位，畢竟，他自己，就是一個閃著金光的珍貴寶塔。

CERS team with Jinta personnel / 中國探險學會與金塔寺人員合影

復興的老靈魂

A HUNDRED YEAR'S OLD
TEA HOUSE REVIVAL

Ya An, Sichuan – June 30, 2023

A HUNDRED YEAR'S OLD TEA HOUSE REVIVAL

"Lao Qi", meaning Old Seven, at 55 years old, is a deaf mute. Not just any handicapped person, but he is at the heart of a documentary by the same name "Lao Qi" which has won six awards at the 15th Morocco Film Festival. Lao Qi has worked at the GuanYinGe (Bodhisattva of Compassion Kiosk) tea house for ten years.

Not just any teahouse dotting every town and city of Sichuan. GuanYinGe is now over a hundred years old, situated in Shuang Liu outside of Chengdu, an ancient tea center by the foothill of the Tibetan plateau. The old-time favor of the teahouse setting, as well as flavor of the tea itself, may have catapulted the fame of this teahouse into the search engine of the internet. Thus forth, Lao Qi himself has become somewhat of a celebrity, a KOL of sorts, with a swarm of followers who come in busloads to photograph the teahouse and Lao Qi.

Such elevated status of Lao Qi is commensurate with the last two decades during which time we saw a huge interest developing in China, going retro about tea drinking. Though the ancient technique and etiquette of tea drinking have largely disappeared in China for decades, it has somehow been maintained as a culture and heritage in Japan, through an exquisite style of tea ceremony. Likewise, tea, fine or packaged to be fine, are exquisite gifts, but speculated to

Stacks of bamboo chairs waiting / 堆叠的竹椅

Tea served in bowls / 碗中奉茶

stratospheric prices. It is considered investment grade to many, not unlike the one-time Dutch tulip bulb bubble. At times, it is even margin on being of shady money laundering value, in the league of painting, orchid, and even a Tibetan mastiff.

With the popularizing of tea culture, many books, articles, films and internet chats began to focus on the Tea-horse caravan of old China. It even got into the pages of the National Geographic as photographed by my old friend and former colleague Michael Yamashita.

It is true that such caravans roamed the foothill to the medium height of the plateau in delivering of tea and other worthy items, before they are transported and relayed onto backs of yaks to gain more height and elevation. But defying common belief, due to the narrow paths and difficult terrain of the Sichuan foothill, horse caravan never gained popularity or practicality out of Ya An going westward. The "Tea-horse Route" and its usage only applied true mainly to the Yunnan stretch of such trade.

Ya An, despite being the tea capital for Tibetan Tea, sometimes called "Ma Cha" or Horse Tea, has not always existed with such high profile. In fact, they are derived from the secondary, or even lowest, quality of tea, yet with the largest scale of production. I first visited such Tibetan tea packaging facilities in 1987 and was amazed at the strong pungent flavor and hard-crushed quality of such tea bricks, bundled up into bales with dried plant fiber, for its long journey into the plateau. By then of course, they are not carried by person, but by truck over low gorges, crossing river torrents and high snowy passes, until it reaches Lhasa and beyond.

Tibetans consider such tea as all essential to their life, just as important as their staple diet of barley. Perhaps the earliest sanction of trade, predecessor of today's overused political sanctions, is the restriction of the Tibetan tea trade going into Tibet during the Qing Dynasty, as a way of punishing the regional government in getting too closed to the British India government. It may have indirectly fostered the growth of Indian tea in the southern Himalayas, subsequently feeding world-renowned hotels and teahouses with the finest brew of Darjeeling, Assam and Sikkim. Long-term sanction often leads to development of alternatives or independence.

As my team and I were staying in Ya An, we decided to beat the tourist crowd and went to GuanYinGe early in the morning, at 7am. But others, the elders of town, were already ahead of us. Almost all the bamboo chairs, traditional to Sichuan, are taken by chatting elders, exclusively men of senior age of a variety with snowy hair, bearded or bald. The wrinkles on their faces perfectly

Chengdu teahouse 1987 / 1987 年的成都茶館

My breakfast & meerschaum pipe /
我的早餐與海泡石菸斗
Old man & his chimey / 老者與他的「煙囪」

match the vintage on the walls of this old teahouse, with the much-faded Cultural Revolution propaganda slogans and pictures painted on its walls.

We chose a corner table and seated ourselves for the tea and bought some local breakfast snacks. The place, despite being with wide open sides, was smoke-filled, with the hard-core elders with cigarettes or pipes. It was particularly so, since we were sitting right next to an older bearded gentleman, puffing like a chimney and peddling his variety of pipes, long or short, making them right from his seat. We felt inclined to buy something from him as well, and soon I too brought out my rarely used white meerschaum pipe and joined the crowd.

Among the tea drinkers, some were playing cards, others a game of Chinese chess or a popular Sichuan game called "Pai Gow" with long cards. Yet others were just chatting and shooting the breezes, enjoying the thin mist of smoke in the air. It is said that the owner of this teahouse, Li Qiang, does not allow playing of mahjong, both because of its noise and also that he felt mahjong in the old days were only for pleasure of the richer families and never part of the tea culture of China. He is probably right in upholding his ethos of perpetuating such ancient tea culture.

Always at hand with his blue apron and serving his customers, we managed to hold him down and be seated with me for a brief interview, after I produced to him a copy of the famous novel "Tea House" authored by my favorite Manchu literati Lao She.

Li Qiang was born in 1965 and now 58 years of age. He was born and grew up in Sichuan at Shuangliu's Pengzhen where we are, and much affected by the tea house culture of such little towns. At the time, Pengzhen has only two tea houses, Tea House One and Tea House Two, both government owned and operated. Li's mother started working at Tea House One since the age of 16, whereas Tea House Two is in the exact location of today's GuanYinGe Tea House. Li started hanging around the teahouse since a child and has established emotional ties to the place.

In 1981 at 16, Li started working at a local post office. He did not like the tedious work and quitted in 1985. After a hand in trying different small businesses, including as a fruit vender, he decided to take over the GuanYinGe Teahouse and run it as a continuation of his mother's vocation. After three years, he started to set his price to meet the basic need of the public, at only 30 cents per customer, and has kept that price for the longest time, despite inflation.

Pai Gow card players / 打牌九的人們

Chess players / 象棋玩家

Card players / 打撲克的人

According to Li, site of today's teahouse used to be a small temple built over 300 years ago during the Ming Dynasty. Around 150 years ago, there was a huge fire that burnt down almost all of Pengzhen town, but the temple stayed intact. Town elders thought it must be blessed by the GuanYin deity, and thus it is from then named as GuanYinGe (Ge meaning kiosk). During the early part of the Republic of China Nationalist era, it was turned into a teahouse and lasted until now.

Li opens his shop four in the morning, and closes at eight in the evening. The regular customers are elder men of between 70 to 90, even older. Once they order a bowl of tea, they may stay all day long, heading home only for their meals. Currently, tea per bowl for regular locals is set at One Yuan, defying prices elsewhere throughout China. But for others non-regular guests, it charges Ten Yuan, still way below up-market tea houses anywhere.

Li emphasized that the main difference of his teahouse to others is fairness, fair pricing and fair atmosphere. He felt others set a high entry price, thus establishing a high bar that is not friendly to every class of people, a rather high threshold for class distinction and comparison of affordability. Li felt a traditional teahouse should not have such barriers. For that reason, he could not afford to go through much-needed renovation of the place, and maintained prices irrelevant to the growing cost of the real world in order to keep to his original intent of establishing a truly localized teahouse. I took my hat off for such a utopian idealistic person, sort of a proletariat.

By now, I had been intoxicated by refill after refill of my tea bowl, with my bladder calling for me to *stop. It might as well be since a busload of tourists, all middle-aged women, had just arrived at the scene. Almost two dozen colorfully dress ladies buzzed into the teahouse and began snapping pictures all around us, some with sophisticated cameras, others with mobile phones. My bearded smoking neighbor and his chimney had become the main focus of the click-click(s).*

Soon two ladies started turning to me. Seeing my silver sliver of hair hanging down my cap, one even stepped up to adjust my cap to show more of my long hair. I knew it is time to take leave, though I was fully qualified to pay only One Yuan and stay for the rest of the day. I would gladly let Lao Qi be the star of the show.

Time to leave / 離開的好時機

復興的老靈魂

百年茶館的堅守與情懷

五十五歲的老七是一位聾啞人士。但與一般的聾啞人士不同的是，他是電影《老七》的核心人物。這部以他為原型的影片在第十五屆摩納哥電影節上狂攬六項大獎，向全世界觀眾展示了中國文藝作品特有的人文關懷和黑色幽默。電影把故事場景設定在四川的一個小茶館，而在現實生活中，老七也已經在四川的觀音閣茶館工作十幾年了。

觀音閣不是四川大小城鎮間隨處可見的那種普通茶館。它位於四川成都雙流彭鎮，距今已有一百多年的歷史。近幾年來，這家茶館的古意環境及其茶葉的獨特風味讓其成為了網路上的一大熱門「打卡點」。因此，老七本人也成了某種意義上的「網紅」，粉絲們成車成車地來到這裡，只為一睹茶館與老七的風采。

老七在網路上的火爆，恰逢過去二十年間中國茶文化的復興潮流，人們開始逐漸重拾品茗的傳統。起源於唐朝的「茶道」是茶文化的核心，但已經在中國消失了幾十年，反而被隔壁的日本好好地保留了下來。如今，「茶道」已然被日本人發揚成了一種生活藝術，在中國再復興時也帶上了「高大上」的意味。現在市面上所謂的「精品茶」不過是「魚龍混雜」，奈何它就是有市場，不少人都將其視作極好的禮物，價值時常能炒上天價。還有許多人認為這是一種投資品，於是投資市場裡，茶葉的熱度也不亞於當年由鄂圖曼土耳其引進荷蘭的鬱金香。有時，茶甚至被視為地位等同於藝術品和蘭花的洗錢工具，都快要與我們的西藏獒犬看齊了。

隨著茶文化的普及，許多書籍、文章、電影和網路社交媒體開始關注古老的「茶馬古道」。我的老友兼前同事山下還為美國《國家地理雜誌》拍攝過這一主題。

好像在大家的認知裡，普遍認為古時候這些商隊先是用馬載著茶葉等商品，從山腳下越過蜿蜒崎嶇的山路來到中海拔地區，再把貨品都換到犛牛背上，以便能上到更高的地方。然而事實卻並非如此。由於「蜀道難行」，馬幫一直沒能走出成都之西的雅安，向更西的方向前進。「茶馬古道」其實主要只應用於雲南一帶的貿易中。

雅安，雖被譽為藏茶之鄉，但在我看來，不算名副其實。藏茶有時也被稱為馬茶，但其實這些產自雅安的茶葉質量並不怎麼好，出產規模卻很龐大。一九八七年的時候，我有次參觀了當地的藏茶廠，那種強烈的刺鼻味道和硬實的茶磚實在令我印象深刻。茶磚被捆在乾燥的竹織纖維裡，準備長途跋涉進入高原。彼時運輸已不再過分依賴人力，卡車會帶著它們經過低矮峽谷、橫越湍急的河流和高山埡口，直到抵達拉薩甚至更高更遠的地方。

藏族人視這種茶為生活中不可或缺的一部分，其重要性堪比他們

Early crowd at teahouse / 清晨的茶館人潮
I become a target / 成為被攝對象

Chengdu teahouse circa 1987 /
1987 年前後的成都茶館
Ya An tea brick and bale 1987 /
1987 年雅安生產的茶磚

的主食青稞。其實早在今日屢見不鮮的政治制裁之前，就有了貿易制裁的先例。清朝時期，政府曾嚴格限制過進入西藏的茶葉貿易，目的是懲罰地方政府與英屬印度政府過於親近的行為。這種做法間接促進了南喜馬拉雅地區印度茶的發展，致使如今許多世界知名的酒店和茶館中，大吉嶺、阿薩姆和錫金等印度茶葉占據了重要地位。由此可見，長期的制裁往往會促使替代品的蓬勃發展。

在雅安停留時，我們決定避開遊客潮，起個大早，七點就回去觀音閣。不料鎮上的老一輩已經一步領先，我們趕到時，地道的四川竹椅早已被這些白髮蒼蒼，或留鬍鬚或禿頂的長者們占滿。他們臉上的皺紋與茶館牆上經年失色的文革宣傳口號和畫報相得益彰，彷彿時間在這裡停留。

我們挑了一個角落的桌子坐下，點了些地方特色的早餐小吃，開始品嚐茶香。儘管四周開放，茶館內卻瀰漫著濃濃的煙霧，仔細一看，原來源頭是那些老者嘴邊的香菸和菸斗。特別是坐在我們旁邊的一位留著濃密大鬍子的老先生，他像個煙囪一般地吞雲吐霧，同時不忘展示著他現場製作的各式菸斗，長短不一。我們被這情景吸引，不由自主地也想向他購買幾件。不久後，我甚至拿出了自己罕用的白色海泡石菸斗，試圖融入這分悠閒。

Old man with pipe ware / 拿著菸斗的老人

環顧四周，熙熙攘攘的茶館裡，各式人等自尋樂趣。一角的桌上，牌友們手拿撲克，笑聲不斷；另一邊，兩位老先生聚精會神地對弈中國象棋；幾桌遠外，還有人擺弄著四川特有的長牌「牌九」，場面熱鬧非凡；還有些人，只是聚在一起淡淡地閒聊，在煙霧中半瞇著眼睛，好不自在。關於這家茶館，還有一則趣聞：傳聞老闆李強堅決不允許顧客在此打麻將。一方面，麻將的喧鬧聲會打破這裡的寧靜；另一方面，他認為麻將曾是富家子弟的消遣，並非傳統茶文化的一環。老闆堅守這樣的原則，致力於用自己的方式維護和傳承最原始的茶文化。

身著藍色圍裙，忙碌於迎來送往的李強彷彿一刻也停不下來。在一個難得的空隙，我特意當著他的面拿出我心愛的滿族作家老舍所寫的《茶館》一書，果不其然他眼睛一亮，終於願意坐下來與我進行一次短暫但充滿意義的訪談。

HM presents book to Li /
HM 向老闆李強展示《茶館》書籍

Marked price per bowl / 茶館價目表　Photography detachment of women /
攝影娘子軍

李強生於一九六五年，今年五十八歲。他就在彭鎮長大，這個充滿茶香的小鎮對他的影響深遠。當年，彭鎮僅有兩家茶館，都由政府運營，一家叫「茶館一號」，一家就叫「茶館二號」。李強的母親自十六歲起便在「茶館一號」工作，而「茶館二號」的位置，正是今日觀音閣茶館的所在。從小，李強就在茶館中遊走，對這個地方滋生了深厚的情感。

一九八一年，年僅十六歲的李強在當地郵局找了份工作。他對那枯燥的工作毫無興趣，所以在一九八五年選擇辭職。嘗試過賣水果等多種小本生意之後，他決定接管觀音閣茶館，延續他母親的事業。三年後，他為茶館定下了一個親民的價格，僅收每位顧客茶位費三毛，這個價格在通貨膨脹的壓力下依然堅持到最近。

李強說，今天的茶館原本是一座建於明朝，擁有三百多年歷史的小廟。大約一百五十年前，一場大火幾乎將彭鎮燒為平地，但這座小廟卻奇跡般地完好無損。鎮上的長者們認為這肯定是觀音神明的庇護，於是從那時起，這裡就被命名為觀音閣，「閣」意味著亭。在中華民國初期，這座小廟被改造成了茶館，一直經營至今。

茶館每天從清晨四點開始迎客，直至夜幕降臨的八點才關門。這裡的常客多是七十至九十歲的老先生，甚至有些年歲更高。他們

Chairman Mao / 毛主席畫像
Revolutionary mural / 革命壁畫

Chairman Mao & Li Qiang at counter / 櫃臺的毛主席畫像與李強

一旦點上一碗茶，便可能在這裡坐上一整天，晚上用餐時才匆匆回家。今日，對於當地的熟客，一碗茶仍然只需一元人民幣，在全中國的茶市中可謂獨一無二。而對於偶爾光顧的非常客，每碗茶收費十元，這個價格在遍地「高端茶館」的今天也是十分親民了。

李強特別強調，他的茶館，核心在於「公平」：無論是公正的價格還是平等的氛圍，皆為鎮館之本。他認為，其他茶館設下的高門檻價格，無形中劃出了階級的界限，而階級差異是社會永遠的痛點。在李強看來，一間承載傳統精神的茶館，理應拒絕這樣的隔閡。因此，即便是茶館已迫切需要翻新，他也堅持用舊時的價格，不隨世界成本上揚，以守住創建一個真正屬於本土的茶館的初心。對這位有著「烏托邦」理想的人，我打心眼裡向他致敬，這才是真正的普羅大眾的平凡英雄。

此時，我已被一波波的茶香淹沒，滿腹茶意讓我幾乎忘記了時間的流逝，但我膀胱發出的警告實在有點不容忽視。正在此時，一車中年女士的到來打破了寧靜。她們穿著與茶館色調反差明顯的五彩衣裳，蜂擁而入，開始在四處留下快門的喀嚓聲。我的大鬍鬚鄰居和他那如煙囪般的菸斗，很自然地成為了她們鏡頭下的焦點。

不久後，她們注意到了我帽子下隨性的銀白長髮，於是又將目光轉向了我。一位女士甚至走上前來，輕柔地調整我的帽子，讓我的長髮更加引人注目。此時，我明白該是離開的時候了，儘管我已經付了一元錢，有資格在這裡悠哉地享受一整個下午。但是低調如我，怎麼能搶別人的風頭呢，還是讓老七去當這場秀的主角吧！

國王與乞丐

KING AND THE PAUPER

Thimphu, Bhutan – Sept 2, 2023

KING AND THE PAUPER

"Happy birthday, a bit belated!" said the King as we shook hands and exchanged greetings. "My grandmother told me that she hosted your birthday lunch yesterday at her palace, so I want to stop by to wish you a happy birthday, too," the King continued. King Jigme Khesar Wangchuck is the 5th and current King of Bhutan. His father, the 4th King, abdicated eighteen years ago and passed the mantle to his son, now 43 years of age.

Mark Twain may have written his renowned story, the Prince and the Pauper, as fiction. But for me it seems what happened today was a real-life parallel, though the prince has been upgraded to a king. While not a pauper myself, I am considered a commoner here, and yet the King dropped by my hotel and we chatted for two hours while sipping coffee.

I was only given an hour notice before his arrival, just as I sat down to have tea at Namseyling, an old palace belonging to Ashi Rani, the late mother of the Royal Grandmother of Bhutan. When I received notice, I quickly returned to my hotel, and soon after the King arrived.

He was driven up quietly, as if on a breeze, in an electric car, seated in the front passenger seat. It had just turned dark and there was no entourage or motorcade nor much security detail. By his side

King with us / 國王與我們

was only his Aide de Camp (ADC) Lieutenant Colonel Lhendup "Toby" Dorji, whose father Benji, the former Chief Justice, I knew well.

The visionary King was more candid than usual. For the first hour we were engaged, the King explained his grand scheme for his kingdom's future, to be formally announced by end of this year. I adlibbed some small talk to enliven and punctuate his more serious plans. My quips included describing my hair-raising experience of flying in the cockpit jump seat of an A320 out of Bhutan in May, as well as the delayed plan of bringing a litter of Tibetan mastiff puppies into Bhutan. I could just see my friend Wendy trying to kick me from under the table to shut me up.

But when the King became more candid, I was also entertained with some small talk on the more personal sides of his life. He did not repeat his story about his love of durian, which he had revealed to me during our last meeting *before the pandemic. I loved the story, though not the fruit. "You know, when we travel overseas and visit a Chinese restaurant, my seven and a half year old son, who reads and speaks Chinese, would do the ordering for us. He started learning Chinese when he was two," said the King. This time, I loved both the story and the food.*

The tidbit about his son the Crown Prince was a nice surprise from the mouth of the King. Despite having a long border with China, the kingdom does not have diplomatic relations with its immediate neighbor. In fact, due in part to political sensitivity and in part to other historical reasons, Bhutan does not have diplomatic relationships with any of the five permanent members of the United Nations Security Council.

"You know I haven't traveled out of my country until quite recently. There is so much to do within Bhutan that I have to care for," said the King. "I went to Philips Exeter and later the UK for education, and once I visited Hong Kong way back in the 1990s," he continued. "But now I must see more places to compare and observe," he quipped as he explained more on how to chart a future plan for the Kingdom, larger than Taiwan or Belgium in size, yet with only 1/30th and 1/15th the population of those two places respectively. In one breathe, he cited many of the neighboring countries and their population sizes from his head as if reading from a book.

The King even revealed something regarding his domestic life: "Her Majesty the Queen will give birth in about ten days or so, and soon after I must resume my travels again." I congratulated him in advance before he took leave, after almost two hours of conversation. While coffee and snacks were served by the hotel, he barely touched it. In parting as he walked to the lobby, he suggested we have a picture taken together, which we gladly obliged. In passing he said : "you know I stayed in this hotel for months during the pandemic. This was my quarantine hotel upon return from making field trips to pacify our people and urge them to take the vaccine shots."

On that note he turned to his ADC and asked : "How long have I quarantined myself at this hotel?" "Seven months in the first year, and six months the next year," came the answer from "Toby". "Ah, each time after my tour of duty, I quarantined for up to 21 days or 14 days. Then I got to go home for two days to hug my kids, and out again immediately," said the King with obvious pride on his face. He did not forget to thank Vic Lee, a CERS Director, who upon request by the Kingdom, at the height of the outbreak of the pandemic, quickly sourced vaccine and other medical equipment before airfreighting them into Bhutan.

A visit and birthday greetings by the King were special enough, but then his grandmother Her Majesty the Royal Grandmother of Bhutan, a most regal royalty at 93 years old, gave me an upgrade. On the day of my birthday, I asked to seek her blessings, by prayers or in person. Instead, I was told that Her Majesty would host a lunch in her palace to celebrate with me. That is not something anyone could even hope for, let alone ask for.

As palace protocol goes, I should not describe details nor take photos of the event. But blessed by Her Majesty, who always made exceptions for me, I usually would prudently select and include some pictures to illustrate my writing for use internally within CERS publications. Her Majesty often asked me to go ahead and take some pictures inside her palace, even of some exquisite art and thangka collections. But I never dared take her generosity for granted.

Her Majesty & How Man at Palace /
皇太后和 HM 在皇宮
Buffet birthday lunch / 生日自助餐

That lunch, a full buffet set out with many dishes, less spicy to accommodate my palate, was most sumptuous. Dessert alone had many choices, but the supreme prize were two birthday cakes, one for me and the other for Wendy, who happened to have the same birthday as me though a year apart. Mine was not just any cake one can order from a bakery. I was born in the Year of the Ox, which I often said makes me a Yak, since I have roamed the Tibetan plateau for decades. The cake was thus specially made with full regalia of three yaks grazing on a green field with three sacred snow mountains behind. In Tibetan and Bhutanese legends these mountains represent the trinity of deities, Jampelyang, Chanadorji and Chenrezig, together being most auspicious. They are the manifestation of compassion, of wisdom and of power respectively. Obviously, some special thought must have been given to the design and making of this cake.

During that lunch, Her Majesty and I had many lovely chats, about early explorers who stayed at her father's home while passing through on their way to Tibet, as well as about the 13th Dalai who stayed at their home for over six months. Of course, all these events happened some eighty or more years ago. Yet Her Majesty remembers every detail as if it happened only yesterday. She even remembers names of several of my directors who visited her back in May this year. I left the palace as always with plenty of gifts from Her Majesty : special health supplements, books, and even a wall

Two birthday cakes / 兩個生日蛋糕

rug given by Ashi Tashi, her sister, who will turn 100 in three days' time.

Little did I know that another birthday surprise was awaiting me that evening. I received several well wishes on my phone during the day. Then after dinner, I received one from Sandra. Sandra has been our CERS Country Manager in Myanmar for eight years. In that country, where recent history has taken many twists and turns, we still maintain two centers, one at Inle Lake and the other near Mandalay. The Mandalay premises near the Irrawaddy River also serve as our HM Explorer exploration boat base. A second building has just been completed, to be set up as a noodle shop in order to help pay for overhead expenses and sustain basic operations into the future.

Sandra sent pictures of our Myanmar team with their birthday wishes, announcing at the same time that they had chosen my birthday for the grand opening of the noodle shop. They prepared two hundred bowls of noodles to serve for free to the villagers living around our site, to celebrate the opening and my birthday. As Chinese believe eating long noodles is synonymous to wishing a long life, this symbolic act was their way of wishing me happy birthday, a most appropriate gift to balance the royal treatment I was given earlier in the day.

I left Bhutan on Drukair flying in an Airbus 320. Soon after I took my seat, an air hostess in beautiful kira came over to greet me. "Captain Choeda would like to invite you to the cockpit," said the lady with a smile. Soon Wendy and I were led into the cockpit. There were two jump seats vacant behind the captain and his co-pilot. Captain Choeda, General Manager of flight operations of Drukair, turned around and shook hands with me and Wendy. Thereupon he showed us the two jump seats and invited us to take up one each. He helped us strap into the shoulder harnesses and seat belts and then turned around to guide his huge plane to the runway.

The thrill of taking off, banking left, then right, and left again as the plane snaked through the mountains of the Himalayas, was beyond words. Soon we were in the clouds, both literally and figuratively. After the plane smoothed off to cruising altitude, we returned to our seats. Everyone was looking bewildered as if wondering where we had disappeared to during take-off. After all, there was only one toilet up front. The lady across the aisle could not resist and asked me.

"Make sure you come to Bhutan for your next birthday," I answered.

Chaw Su preparing noodles / 喬蘇正在煮面

Flying cockpit jump seat out of Bhutan/
乘坐駕駛艙的備用座位離開不丹

國王與乞丐

「雖然有點遲來了，但祝你生日快樂！」年輕的不丹國王一邊與我握手一邊如是說。「我聽說祖母昨天在她的宮殿為你舉辦了生日會，所以我想，我也應該來跟你說聲生日快樂！」吉格梅・凱薩爾・旺楚克是不丹王國的第五任國王，他的父親在十八年前退位，將王位傳給了現年四十三歲的他。

馬克・吐溫的著名的小說《王子與乞丐》或許是純虛構的，但卻神奇地對應上了今天在我身上發生的真實情況，只不過小說中的王子升級成了國王。雖然我不是乞丐，但在這個神祕的不丹王國，我只是一個普通到不能再普通的人。然而此刻，國王卻出現在我住的酒店，與我一邊喝咖啡，一邊暢聊了兩小時。

其實在國王抵達前一小時我才接到通知。當時我正坐在南西嶺皇宮喝茶，那是一座屬於不丹皇太后的母親，拉妮公主的老宮殿。接到通知後，我飛速回到酒店，沒過多久國王便到達了。

他來得非常低調，彼時天色剛剛變暗，他坐在電動汽車前排，無聲無色的到達，周遭沒有浩浩蕩蕩的隨扈車隊或是保安，跟著他的只有一位副官，中校蘭迪普・托比・多吉。有緣的是，這位中校的父親班吉曾是高等法院的首席法官，與我也是舊相識。

那天，這位年輕但充滿遠見的國王顯得比往常更加坦誠。在我們深入交談的第一小時裡，他便向我坦露了他對王國未來的宏大願景，並打算於今年年底正式對外發布一些確切的計畫。這時，談話的氛圍已然有點嚴肅了，所以我打算找一些輕鬆的話題添點生氣。事實上我也真的那麼做了，跟國王興致勃勃地分享了我五月分搭乘 A320 離開不丹時的情景，那次我有幸體驗了一下在駕駛艙裡專屬於飛行員的航空座椅起飛，真是刺激得讓人記憶猶新。我還跟他提起了我那因不可抗力，不得不被疫情延宕的「藏獒幼犬引進不丹計畫」。只不過我一邊說著，一邊默默往後撤了撤雙腿，因為我知道坐在我對面的，我的朋友溫蒂，肯定在找時機踹我，想讓我閉嘴。

事實證明，談話走向更輕鬆時，國王也願意聊起一些我十分愛聽的「私生活」了。他這次沒重複他瘋狂迷戀榴槤那件事了，上次聽他講這個還是在疫情爆發前我們見面那次。我是很喜歡那個故事，但是不喜歡榴槤。「你知道嗎，我兒子七歲半了，他從兩歲開始就學習中文了，上次我們出國旅行去中餐館吃飯時，他能用中文替我們點餐。」聽到這個新故事，我又驚又喜，這次我是既喜歡那食物，也喜歡故事。

雖然不丹與中國接壤的邊界長達四百七十多公里，但它跟中國這樣的近鄰卻沒有邦交。事實上，由於政治敏感性和一些歷史因素，

Namseyling Palace / 南西嶺皇宮
Hotel Zhiwaling / 我入住的織瓦靈飯店

Two birthday cakes / 兩個生日蛋糕

不丹甚至與聯合國安全理事會的五個常任理事國都沒有建立外交關係。

「其實我有好些年都沒有出過國了，直到最近才開始到處走動走動。因為不丹內部有太多事情，必須我親自盯著。」國王說。「我以前在菲利普斯艾希特學院上過學（美國的私立貴族高中，名作家丹布朗的母校），後來又去英國唸書，九〇年代還曾去過香港一次。」他繼續說。「不過現在，我必須去到更多國家和地區以作比較和觀察，這是我的使命。」他談到如何為王國制定未來計畫時打趣說道，不丹王國的面積比台灣和比利時都大，但人口分別只有它們的三十分之一和十五分之一。他就這樣一口氣提到了許多鄰國及其人口數據，熟練得彷彿是照著書本上讀出來的一樣。

國王甚至透露了一些關於他家庭生活的事情。「王后大約再過十天就要臨盆了，但我也不能陪伴她太久，馬上就又得啟程，繼續出國考察。」聽及此，我提前向他表示祝賀，然後在近兩小時的對話後，他告辭離開。酒店給我們提供了咖啡和精美的點心，但他幾乎沒碰。告別時他走到大廳，建議我們一起合影留念，我們當然樂意至極。他順便說道：「疫情期間我在這家酒店住過幾個月，當時是剛從國內各地考察回來，在這裡隔離，為的是給我的人民們做個示範、安撫他們一下，並敦促他們接種疫苗。」

他轉向副官問道：「你還記得我在這家酒店隔離了多久嗎？」「第一年總共七個月，第二年有六個月。」副官回答道。「啊真的是，每次出差結束後，我都得隔離十四天到二十一天，然後能回家兩天抱抱孩子，馬上又得出發。」聽起來是有點令人煩惱的狀況，但國王說起卻是滿臉的自豪。他還沒忘記鄭重感謝 CERS 的理事 Vic Lee。Vic 曾在疫情爆發高峰期迅速採購了疫苗和其他醫療設備，馬不停蹄地空運到不丹。

Royal gifts / 來自不丹皇室的禮物
Mango from 4th king's farm / 四代國王農場的芒果

其實國王的親自探訪和生日祝福已經夠令我倍感榮幸了，但他的祖母，不丹的皇太后，一位九十三歲的尊貴皇族，才實在是讓我受寵若驚。在我生日的當天，我厚著臉皮向她討祝福，想著她要是能親口說一句祝福語或是幫我做個禱告我都太感激了。所以，可想而知，當我得知皇太后陛下將在她的宮殿裡為我舉辦一場生日會，共進午餐，慶祝生日時，我該是多麼驚喜。這哪是我敢指望的事呀，我想任何人都不敢要求這種待遇吧！

其實按照宮廷的嚴謹禮儀，我本不應流露半點細節的，更別說拍什麼照片了。但是，尊貴的皇太后陛下總是為我單獨開綠燈，她甚至經常跟我說，讓我放心大膽地在宮殿裡拍就好了，如果願意的話也可以多拍拍那些精美的藝術品和唐卡收藏。雖說如此，我也從不敢把她的慷慨善良當做理所應當。所以每次為 CERS 出版物寫關於不丹的與王室有關的插圖時，我都是抱著前所未有的謹慎態度去精挑細選。

那一頓生日宴，餐桌上擺滿了形形色色的佳餚，為迎合我的口味，還特別做得不是很辣，我是真真看花了眼。甜品選擇繁多，但當天的最高榮譽非兩個生日蛋糕莫屬，一個是屬於我的，另一個則是為與我同日生日的溫蒂準備的，我和我的「有緣人」溫蒂生日相同，只是年分上差一歲。我的蛋糕非同一般，不是吹「牛」，絕對是任何一家烘焙店都做不出的。那塊蛋糕上有一幅栩栩如生的立體圖案，雕塑出三隻犛牛在翠綠的草地上悠閒地吃著草，背後則是三座聳立的神山，象徵著藏族和不丹傳說中的三大神祇——代表慈悲的觀自在、智慧的文殊，以及力量的金剛手，三者的聚集預示著極大的吉祥。我經常說我自己就是犛牛，因為出生在牛年，又數十年來遊走於青藏高原。那時我望著那塊充滿了特殊含義的蛋糕，內心的感激之情無以言表。

生日會上，皇太后還跟我聊了許多趣事兒。從早年的探險家們在前往西藏途中曾暫留她父親府邸，講到第十三世達賴喇嘛也曾在她家逗留過六個多月。這些往事雖已逾八十年，但陛下對每一個細節的記憶卻彷彿歷歷在目，好像是昨天剛剛發生的事，她甚至還清楚地記得今年五月來訪的我的幾位董事們的名字，由此可見她的記憶力有多厲害。每次離開宮殿，我總是帶著陛下送的大大小小的禮物「滿載而歸」。這次不僅有皇家特製的保健品、書籍，還有陛下的姊姊塔希公主送的珍貴掛毯，這位塔西公主將在三天後迎來百歲的壽辰。

那天晚上之前，我還不知道有另一個生日驚喜在等著我。整日裡，遠方的祝福讓我的手機響個不停，而就在晚餐後，珊卓的祝福也如約而至。珊卓是我們緬甸的項目主管，

Wendy at buffet table / 正在挑選食物的溫蒂

Palace birthday lunch / 皇宮午餐
Noodle shop opening / 當日開張的緬甸麵館

已經為學會工作八年了。如今在這個動盪的國家，我們依舊努力維持著兩個中心，一個在茵萊湖畔，另一個在靠近伊洛瓦底江的曼德勒，那裡也是我們的探險船「HM 探險家號」的停靠基地。最近，我們在曼德勒地區的第二棟建築剛剛竣工，按計畫是想把它做成一個麵店，這樣能為緬甸區的項目提供些資金支持。

點開手機，看到珊卓寄來的我們緬甸團隊的合照，心裡不免暖洋洋的。然而更令我驚喜的是，他們特意把麵店開張的日子選在了我生日這天。為了慶祝這個日子，他們還精心準備了兩百碗麵條，免費發放給中心周圍的村民，讓大家一起快樂快樂。中國人素來有生日吃麵條的習俗，因為信奉著長麵代表長壽，我知道，她們是真的有心了。這份禮物對我來說再好不過，因為我從小被教導，接受的同時一定要懂得施與，緬甸同事們的這種方式，恰好幫我把從不丹皇室那裡接收到的善意給予了更多的人。

這次離開不丹，我搭乘的是空中巴士 A320。剛坐下不久，一位空姐身著美麗的不丹傳統長裙「旗拉」走了過來，微笑著說：「丘達機長想請您到駕駛艙去。」於是，我與溫蒂被帶進駕駛艙，機長和副駕駛後方有兩個空置的折疊座椅。丘達機長轉過身來與我和溫蒂握手，邀請我們各自坐下。他幫我們繫好安全帶，然後轉身利落地駕著他的巨型飛機滑向跑道。

當飛機在喜馬拉雅山脈間穿梭，左右擺動時，從駕駛室看出去的那種刺激真是難以言喻。不久，我們便真真切切地進入了雲層，周遭白茫茫的一片，這下真是應了那句成語「騰雲駕霧」了。直到飛機進入巡航高度平穩下來後，我們才回到乘客座位上。周圍的乘客一臉疑惑，好像都在猜想我們在起飛期間去了哪裡。畢竟，表面上前面只有一個洗手間。走道對面的外籍女士實在沒忍住，開口問了我。

「下次過生日的時候來不丹吧，到時你就知道了。」我笑著回答。

CERS Myanmar core team / CERS 緬甸團隊

我的《國家地理雜誌》歲月

MY DAYS AT THE NATIONAL GEOGRAPHIC

Hong Kong – Sept 20, 2023

MY DAYS AT THE NATIONAL GEOGRAPHIC

The words National Geographic, for people all over the world, conjure up the image of a yellow-bordered magazine with excellent pictures of our physical world on every page. For over a hundred and thirty years, since the magazine was founded in 1888, it has been a fixture in many homes and libraries.

In fact, for over a decade of its early existence, the magazine had hardly any photographs but existed largely as a scientific journal. The first full pictorial article was published in 1904; a story on Lhasa submitted by the Imperial Russian Geographical Society of St. Petersburg. The pictures were taken by the Buryat-Buddhist explorer Gombozhab Tsybikoff, originally from Russian central Asia. (It was his presence in Lhasa that precipitated the British Younghusband military invasion of Tibet.) The editor of the magazine at the time used Tsybikoff's pictures to fill the empty pages when he lacked enough text stories. He expected he might be fired for substituting photos for text but was instead praised for his decision. That became a beginning that shaped the subsequent decades' monumental growth and a following century when the magazine came to be the standard for visual reporting of our world, and in time even of the universe, illustrated by pictures first and foremost, supplemented by captions and text.

My own journey at National Geographic is more personal, beginning with my early years as a journalist. Trained as a writer, with a double major at the University of Wisconsin in Journalism and Art, I found the opportunity to begin working in China in 1974 independently. By 1981, my sojourns had taken me into some of the most remote regions of China, areas populated by little known ethnic minorities. A chance meeting with a top photo agency in New York landed me an introduction and I found myself at the doorstep of Mary Smith, Senior Editor at the National Geographic.

Mary was used to working with the leading explorer-scholars of the day including Jacque Cousteau, Louis Leakey, George Schaller, Dian Fossey, Jane Goodall, etc. She saw the potential for not only a single story for the magazine, but for an ongoing cooperation in support of my pioneering exploration in China. Thus began a journey that led to my six major expeditions over the next few years. The building at 17th & M Street, headquarters of the National Geographic, became my home away from home. Flying first class and staying at five-star hotels with an "unlimited" budget was the norm the magazine provided for its top explorer/journalists in those days.

In time, Bill Garrett, Editor in Chief, Bob Gilka, Director of Photography, and Bill Graves, my text editor, all became my close friends and chief

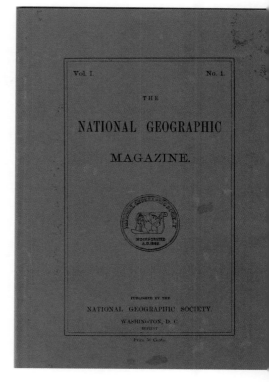

Cover of 1888 / 創刊號封面

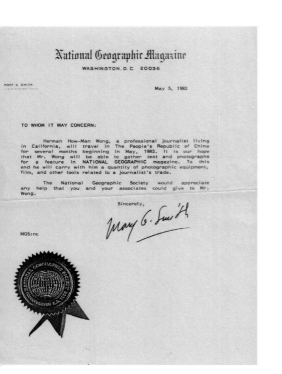

Letter of Intro 1982 / 1982 年的介紹信

supporters of my work. I remember Bob Gilka's door mat into his office: "Wipe your knees before entering," testifying to the aura and huge budget under his watch. "Do not take up sponsorship. If make sense and needed, buy it," said Gilka to me. Thus on my Yangtze expedition between 1985 to 1986, I bought a Four-wheel Drive Landcruiser, two Zodiac boats with outboard motors, one off-road motorcycle, and three mountainbikes, besides a long list of other equipment. His support, as well as that of Bill Garrett, was both substantial and crucial, allowing me to roam free and explore vast tracts of China little known to the outside world. It was at a time when the magazine was at its prime, with over 11 million subscribers globally (the first issue in 1888 listed 205 members). It was also a time when old school photojournalism was having its heyday, based on the use of still photographs taken with slide transparencies.

For National Geographic photographers in those days, each was an elite among elites, rising to the pantheon of photojournalism. When they travel, they were likely to bring a lot of cameras, film and related equipment, hire a fixer, an interpreter and a car and driver, and then off they went for a few weeks on assignment. For a writer, they carried much less, perhaps just a notebook and a pen. But to be on expedition and explore in remote areas, the amount of preparation was immense. I remember loading up an entire airplane container a day before departure with over thirty pieces

Off-road vehicle and motorcycle / 越野車和摩托車
Inflatable boat and motor / 充氣艇與馬達

of luggage, which included an inflatable boat, outboard motor with several spare propellers, gas tanks and engine oil, an off-road motorcycle, two mountain bikes, tents, sleeping bags, provision of months' supply of freeze-dried food, spare parts for cars down to bearings and many spare tires and inner tubes. Just the list of medical supplies stretched to four pages. Not to speak of the Land Cruiser that had to be purchased and delivered. Recounting the logistics and paperwork to bring all these exotic goods into China through customs clearance at that time would mean reliving a most painful ordeal.

My motto was that it was easier to ask for forgiveness than for permission. This worked both in the field in China as well as back in the accounts office at National Geographic headquarters. The trick was - deliver results. The results of two of my six expeditions for National Geographic became an unprecedented 52-page story on China in the magazine and subsequently yielded two additional books. Those expeditions culminated in the Yangtze Expedition, spread over three successive journeys between 1985 and 1986. The feather in my cap was defining a new and longer source for that mighty river. Such expeditions not only honed my skills for more geographic exploration and quest for knowledge, they also started me on a life-long career path that led me to create the China Exploration & Research Society (CERS) in 1986. After that, we added several more feathers to the cap by defining the sources of the Mekong, Yellow, Salween, Irrawaddy and Brahmaputra Rivers, all under auspices of CERS.

The world has changed much since those days. In China, even the distant provinces and autonomous regions I used to roam have become easily accessible. Our insider joke at the National Geographic was that we were like Playboy Magazine, "showing you all the places you cannot get into." Such jokes may have become unacceptable in this age of sensitivity, eclipsed by the times, like the printed magazine itself. Be that as it may, I continue the journey and explore far beyond the boundaries of China, into Southeast Asia and much of the world.

CERS will soon enter its fourth decade of existence, now with a legacy of expeditions, centers and project sites spanning multiple countries of Asia. We carry on fulfilling the original mission of the founders of the National Geographic to increase and diffuse geographical knowledge, but we are also fostering a new mission of inspiring future generations, promoting the spirit of exploration in research, in conservation, and in life.

Everyone is born with the spirit of exploration, but some of the qualities of an explorer cannot be groomed, they are innate. Eccentricity is certainly one. I remember riding the express elevator with Bill Garrett, the Editor-in-Chief of National Geographic, up to the 10th floor for lunch, where a long table decorated with the flags of both America and China was set up to honor the return of an explorer from the field.

I was, at the time, 33 years of age!

Photo equipment et al / 滿地的攝影器材   Airplane container / 裝得滿滿的空運貨櫃   More equipment / 多到不行的設備

我的《國家地理雜誌》歲月

相信提到《國家地理雜誌》這幾個大字，大家的第一印象總是那本封皮是黃色邊框的，每一頁都印著無與倫比照片的精美圖書。自從一八八八年創刊以來，逾過一百三十年的歲月，它早已成為許多家庭和圖書館中一份不可或缺的珍藏品。

但其實，在創立初期十餘年的時間裡，《國家地理雜誌》內頁幾乎沒有什麼照片，它本身主要是以科學期刊的面貌存在。直到一九〇四年，第一篇圖文並茂的文章才華麗登場，那是由聖彼得堡的皇家俄羅斯地理學會所投稿的一篇關於拉薩的故事。照片由來自俄羅斯中亞布里亞特地區的佛教探險家貢博扎布・崔比科夫拍攝。彼時也正是由於他出現在拉薩，間接引發了第二次英國侵藏戰爭。當時的雜誌編輯因文字報導篇幅不夠，隨即用崔比科夫的照片來填補空頁。這本是個無奈之舉，編輯也戰戰兢兢地擔心自己會丟掉飯碗，卻不料無心插柳柳成蔭，這個決定成了備受好評的「創舉」。從此，一場跨世紀的，聲勢浩大的「藝術革命」開始了。在之後數十年的飛速發展中，《國家地理雜誌》逐漸成為了全球視覺報導的標準。一篇稱得上優秀的報導，從此基本都是先呈現重要的照片，再搭配標題和文字說明，這樣的模式可謂是歷久不衰。

我的《國家地理雜誌》之旅，與我豐富的個人情感交雜在一起，始於我身為記者的青蔥歲月。在威斯康辛大學接受新聞與藝術雙修的磨練之時，我主要是希望以作家的身分打磨自己。一九七四年，一個偶然的機遇使我能獨立到中國工作，到了一九八一年，我的腳步已經踏過了許多中國最遙遠的角落，有時我會覺得，在那些鮮為人知的少數民族聚居區的時光，重新塑造了我的一小部分靈魂。後來，我在紐約無意間結識了一個頂尖的攝影機構，在他們的牽線搭橋下，某一天，我驚喜地發現自己站在了《國家地理雜誌》資深編輯，瑪麗·史密斯的門前。

瑪麗慣於與當時頂尖的探險家合作，其中包括雅克·庫斯托（法國探險家兼水肺發明者）、路易斯·李奇（英國考古學家兼人類學家）、喬治·夏勒（美國動物學家）、黛安·佛西（美國靈長類動物學家）和珍·古德（英國生物學家兼著名保育人士）等人。她的眼光總是尖銳的。她認為，在我身上投資所能帶來的回報絕不僅僅只是雜誌上的一則熱門故事，於是她決定與我進行長期合作，支持我在中國的深度探索。就這樣，我開始了一段不僅於我個人而言意義重大的旅程，在未來的幾年時間裡，我帶隊進行了六次大型探險活動。《國家地理雜誌》位於第十七街與 M 街交界處的大樓，成了我遠離家居的第二個家。出行都是頭等艙，住五星級酒店，不用過多考慮資金限制因為拿到的是「無限」預算。這些都是雜誌給予其頂尖探險記者的支持。我還買了越野車和充氣快艇，為我的探險隊伍補足裝備。

隨著時間的推移，我與我的主編比爾·加勒特、攝影總監鮑勃·

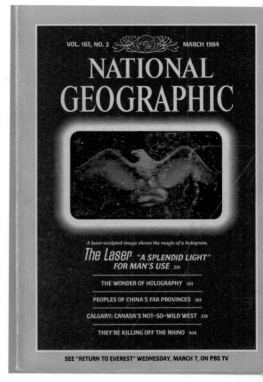

Yellow-bordered magazine / 經典黃框雜誌

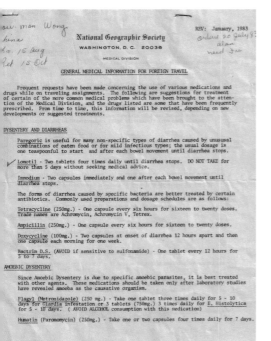

Medical check-list / 醫藥品清單

吉爾卡、以及文字編輯比爾·格雷夫斯都處成了互相支持、親密無間的「戰友」。我還記得鮑勃·吉爾卡辦公室門墊上的個性留言：「進門前請把膝蓋擦乾淨。」真的是「錢多人膽大」。但絕對不可否認的，也是我非常感激的一點是，沒有他和比爾·加勒特各個方面的支持，我是不可能如此自由地去探索外界鮮為人知的中國廣袤土地的，他們是我多次成功探險的堅強後盾和不可或缺的因素。那是《國家地理雜誌》的全盛時期，全球訂閱者從一八八八年第一期的兩百零五名創辦會員增長到了超過一千一百萬人。那時也正是老派攝影新聞學如日中天的時代，一張張透明底片彰顯著攝影資源的珍貴。我的座右銘是：「事後求原諒總是容易過事先求許可。」這一策略無論是在中國的野外還是美國總部的會計辦公室都行之有效。當然這招也是有訣竅的，那就是得帶上你漂亮的成果當「說客」。

那個時代《國家地理雜誌》麾下的攝影師，每一個都是精英中的佼佼者，稱得上是新聞攝影殿堂裡的眾神。數位技術不發達的年代，他們出差要準備的東西可比現在複雜得多。一堆相機、膠卷是基礎，其他相關裝備多到得雇用一名助理，通常還需要一名翻譯和一輛車，這樣一出任務就是好幾週。對於作家來說，要帶的東西就少多了，只需一個本子和一支筆。但要在偏遠地區進行探險，準備工作還是多到不行。記得有次出發前一天清算時發現，我們一行三人加起來總共有三十多件行李，多到裝滿了一整個飛機貨櫃。其中包括一艘充氣船、帶幾個備用螺旋槳的外板馬達、油桶和機油、一輛越野摩托車、兩輛山地自行車、帳篷、睡袋、夠吃三個月的冷凍食品，還有軸承，備用輪胎和內胎的汽車零件。前面提到的這些還遠不是我那滿滿當當物品清單上的全部，具象化點來說，清單上光是醫療用品就寫滿了四頁紙，更別提我們還得帶上兩輛豐田越野車。那時出一次差的繁瑣程度現在再回想起來都頭疼，把那所有東西清關帶入中國要做的後勤和文書工作真的再也不想經歷一次了。

在我帶隊進行的六次大型探險活動中，頭兩次便已成果卓著，成為《國家地理雜誌》中前所未有的五十二頁中國特輯和其後探險的兩本專著。其中我最引以為傲的成就，是跨越一九八五至一九八六年間，考察長江從出海口到源頭的三次遠征。在我們重新定義了那條雄偉河流新源頭的時刻，我自豪的心情實在難以言喻。這些遠征不僅磨練了我地理方面的專業技能，也在精神層面上深刻地塑造了我，我開始比以往更加渴望對知識的追求，也因此，啟發了我之後為之奮鬥一生的探險事業。離開《國家地理雜誌》後，我於一九八六年創立了中國探險學會 CERS。此後，CERS 一步步身體力行著「飲水思源」，依次確定了湄公河、黃河、瀾滄江、伊洛瓦底江和雅魯藏布江的源頭，為我們江河源頭探險的記事簿上又增添了許多光彩。

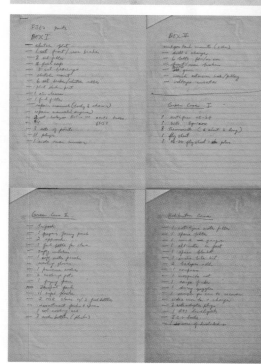

Equipment list / 裝備清單
Car parts check-list / 汽車零件清單

HM on reindeer 1983 / 1983 年 HM 在東北

HM go hunting 1984 / 1984 年 HM 正在打獵

時過境遷，從前的日子遠去，世界已然變化許多。在中國，那些我曾跨越萬里迢迢江水的阻攔才能到達的偏遠地區，如今已變得觸手可及。有些東西已經變得徹底，就像《國家地理雜誌》從前最受歡迎的內部的笑話，在如今這個敏感的年代已經不被接受，只能如同紙本雜誌一般悄然退場。我反正還是覺得那則笑話很經典：「我們就像《花花公子》雜誌一樣，讓你看的全是你進不去的地方。」但不管怎麼樣，我依然是步履不停，甚至後來的探索範圍遠超過中國邊界。

如今 CERS 即將進入其成立的第四個十年，我們的足跡已遍布亞洲多國。我始終記得《國家地理雜誌》創始人的初衷，去不斷地增進和傳播地理知識，同時，還要兼顧激勵後代、推廣探索，研究，保育文化精神的使命。

每個人天生都有探險精神，但探險家卻不是人人都能當的。你得有點異於常人的個性。記得有次，我和我的主編比爾‧加勒特一起乘坐專用電梯直達總部大樓的十樓用餐。華麗的長桌上，美國和中國的國旗挨在一起，歡迎著從野外凱旋而歸的探險家。彼時我才三十三歲，快速上升帶來耳膜膨脹的眩暈感還未完全消退。望著腳下寬廣的一切，我卻從未覺得我踩在世界之上，我只是在沉思，該怎樣用我的一生去盡力擁抱這個世界。

1985 Yangtze glacier source / 1985 年長江源頭
1985 HM with horse / 1985 年 HM 與他的馬兒

踏雪披霜的西伯利亞奇行錄　第一章

WINTER EXPEDITION TO SIBERIA (Part 1)

Russia Siberia Far East – Nov 26 to Dec 7, 2023

WINTER EXPEDITION TO SIBERIA (Part 1)
Crossing the Amur into Russia

I am in the midst of an ocean of snow. Texting home with images of where I am now has some redeeming value. With the temperature dropping below minus twenty, it may also drop a few jaws. Announcing that we are not really in Russia but rather in Siberia would add some sense of mystery. Siberia for me is both a geographical and political term, of wilderness and of exile, let alone implying the depth of a Siberian winter. The crossing of the hard frozen Amur River (Heilong Jiang) is just as exceptional; via hovercrafts sliding left and right as if waltzing, until finally we arrive on the north bank some 700 meters away. Each round takes around twenty people. Immigration and customs are the only things that are routine; waiting in line that is.

The bitter cold outside contrasts with the warm reception we receive in Blagoveshchensk. The Russian city across the Amur River from Heihe on the Chinese side is as hard in spelling and pronunciation as the frozen river. Though it is in the Siberian Far East, it is very European as well. The colorful high-domed Orthodox churches help set the scene among other European style buildings, some lit up at night. Having a cloak room at every restaurant with a courteous concierge is another example of European culture. We hand over our heavy down coats to a lady in attendance at the Smoke and Grill, a posh restaurant inside a brand-new building by the river front, said to be the most expensive property in the city.

Forward come two middle-aged gentlemen greeting us, Boris Leonidovich Belpborodov and Gennady Vladimirovich Illarionov. If the city name is difficult, people's names are hopeless. Both of my hosts are Russians living in Siberia, yet it is not unusual to run into Russians with Asian features. Mikhail, our young interpreter/guide, is one such person with an Asian face, hailing from the circumpolar city of Yakutsk. And bless him for coming with a much shorter last name – Ivanov - since we will be attached to him for the next two weeks. Mikhail is a recent graduate in philosophy from Moscow National University and has traveled widely in Europe and Asia, a rather affluent yet courteous young fellow.

Boris is chairman of the Russian-Chinese People's Friendship Association, and Gennady is Chairman of the Russian Geographical Society (RGS) Amur branch. The former organization is newly formed here in this frontier city, whereas the RGS was first founded in 1845 under the Czar as the Russian Imperial Geographical Society. Later its prefix was amended to "USSR" and then to just "Russian". Its chairman is not regular person nor

HM in thick clothing / 穿著厚重衣服的 HM
Ice flower / 雪花

a scholar - Putin. Before dinner, we are shown a film depicting Siberia's natural beauty, naturally shot during the summer rather than winter. It includes many aerial scenes taken by drone. The dinner is sumptuous, with steak and grilled fish, tasty sausages and finally my first authentic bortsch soup served Russian style. As for beverage, I am glad we are served some fine wine rather than the high-octane vodka, a staple beverage across the arctic north.

Word of our team of six's visit must have gotten spread through the grapevine. The scanty information online about CERS and myself seems adequate to open doors in this faraway corner. They even know the latest news; that the University of Hong Kong has opened a Wong How Man Centre for Exploration. So, I am not treated as a tourist, and our reception is more formal than expected.

We are informed that, for the following days, our itinerary has been changed - or rather overhauled.

Russian Coke with meal in Siberia /
在西伯利亞美食和俄羅斯版可口可樂

Addiction retro / 「倒版」麥當勞

First, we shall visit the Svobodny Arboretum. The next couple of days' full program will then start with a visit to the local Amur State University, and they expect me to deliver a talk to the students, followed by TV interview and another lecture. Everything becomes impromptu, despite that my usual lectures and television interviews are planned weeks or months ahead. It crosses my mind that our importance may have been escalated by the international sanctions put upon Russia at this particular time. Even Coca-Cola has left Russia and my favorite drink has now been replaced by a local concoction tasting and looking quite similar. My addiction to McDonald's is fulfilled by restaurants that have turned the Golden Arches up-side-down, copied even by burger joints on the Chinese side of the border.

I know too little about Siberia to plan my own itinerary across the border. The only instructions I gave to our handler was that we are not tourists and have no intention of becoming such. So now I am treated with some pomp while being expected to perform. Always so very independent in planning my trips, I cannot help feeling like a pawn being moved on a chessboard by some champion Russian chess player. I fear that the next game may be Russian roulette when we tread on thin ice, as I hear that ice fishing over the Amur River has been added to our itinerary. Yet somehow it all seems reassuring, as I can feel the warmth and goodwill; thus I resign myself to their planning.

We spend almost all day in the cold heading to the faraway Svobodny some 150 kilometers out of town. It is a frontier-like town with many wooden homestead houses. Svobodny was once a major Gulag community with over 200,000 exiles doing forced labor during the time of construction of the Transiberian Railway. Today, it has around a quarter of its former population. Visiting a botanical garden covered under snow is another first for me. I dutifully make the rounds through some tall pine and fir forest, hoping such a visit is not a forewarning. The arboretum, a forest scientific experimental station, was made famous by Ivan Michurin, a Russian naturalist with a specialty in botany, and his bust statue sits near the entrance. He is said to have bred more than 300 new varieties of berry and fruit crops. While I do not see the famous Siberian flying squirrel, I do see a squirrel with fluffy tasseled ears. This one looks exactly like the Abert's tassel-eared squirrels of the America southwest, as if somehow it made its way as an immigrant from the New World to the Old. But it is a dark morph of the Eurasian Red Squirrel, and I can see some red tufts above the ear.

On our way back, we stop to look at a lady by the roadside selling home-made fruit wine and freshly caught fish, mainly pike out of the Amur River. Olesya's shop is a trailer parked on the roadside with the frozen fish hanging outside with prices marked. I buy a pike that is half a meter long for a meager 800 rubles (USD$9). Having no place to cook it, it ends up going home with Boris after our Chinese dinner.

As return of the grace given us, I invite our host to a Chinese dinner that evening, feeling that at least I can finally read the menu and know how to pick dishes. The best place in town is said to be a hotpot joint entered through a side door with two lanterns in a new commercial building. Fortunately, we have made reservations earlier, as the entire restaurant is full of local Russians. The menu provides rather popular dishes like sweet and sour pork, and so on and so forth. All the waitresses are Russian. We go up to the counter to have a chat and ask to see the chef, expecting him to be Chinese. Our request is politely turned down, but we do find out there is not one Chinese in the entire place, as the chef and cooks are all Russian, likewise the owner.

Olesya trailer shop / 奧列西婭的小攤

On the following day, my host at the university is Valentina, head of the Department of International Business. She walks me through a couple of buildings before we settle in a large classroom where some fifty to sixty students have converged and are quietly seated. As these are first year students studying Chinese, I end up speaking in English while Mikhail performs simultaneous translation. The highlight is not the lecture itself nor the ending film. When I finish speaking, these young students crowd up front asking for autographs in their notebooks - some even produce pieces of paper for me to sign. I suddenly feel like a superstar.

In the afternoon, we are taken to the Regional Scientific Library for a television interview for a fifteen-minute program. Dana Chernysheva, anchor of Russian Channel 24, asks some interesting questions, especially related to river sources of Asia that my team reached over the years. I explain to her that, for me, the two main focus areas of Siberia are also river related. The first is the Lena River, flowing north from Lake Baikal and draining into the Arctic Ocean, being the 11th longest river in the world. The other is the Amur River where we are, which defines much of the national border of China and Russia. We hope to explore these two river systems in the coming years. I assume the interview is aired the same evening since we receive a link of the broadcast the following day. Our activities are also quickly posted on the Geographical Society website, showing how efficient our hosts are.

Right after the interview, I am ushered into another lecture room where around eighty people, mainly elders, are seated. These are members of the local chapter of the Russian Geographical

Society. Among them there are maybe twenty or so younger people. Women seem to outnumber men by four to one.

The lecture must have been well received, as judged from the enthusiasm of the audience crowding up front to get a photo op before we have to leave for the train station for an overnight train to our next destination, where ice fishing and more are waiting for us.

As the train rolls out of the station in darkness, the rhythmic sound of its wheels brings back to mind the familiar deep solo voice and chorus of "Song of the Volga Boatman". But my mind keeps also going back to the bitter hardship of those who braved to open this railway passage from Europe all the way to the farthest seacoast in the Far East. I gradually fall asleep in the warmth of my bunk while admiring the perseverance of such a people. For the moment, politics becomes just an asterisk in a sentence, not even a paragraph, a chapter, a book or a magnum opus for a people.

Boris & Gennady Chinese restaurant / 鮑里斯和根納季在中國餐館

Zhang Fan speaks at university / 張帆在大學演講

HM autographing / 明星 HM 正簽名

踏雪披霜的西伯利亞奇行錄 第一章 橫穿阿穆爾河進入俄羅斯

現在我正置身於一片無垠的雪海之中。在零下二十多度的氣溫下拍兩張照發回家，足以讓親朋好友驚掉下巴。尤其當我告知他們，我其實不在俄羅斯，而是在西伯利亞，就顯得這趟旅程更加神祕了。對我來說，西伯利亞既是地理名詞、也是政治術語，象徵著荒野和流放，尤其現在是深邃的寒冬，光是看著這個名詞就已經能感覺到冰霜刺骨了。阿穆爾河，也就是中國的黑龍江。這次我們要穿越冰封的河面到達對岸的俄羅斯，想想就刺激。每次只能載二十人左右的氣墊船在冰面上左搖右晃，好像在跳恰恰舞一樣，最終將我們送到七百米外的北岸。整體來說，坐船滑冰入境還是很絲滑的，船程不到二十分鐘，剩下的海關手續就是例行公事，排隊等候罷了。

苦寒的天氣與我們在布拉戈維申斯克受到的熱情接待形成鮮明對比。這座俄羅斯城市位於黑龍江黑河市對岸，名字的拼寫和發音如同它面前冰封的河水一樣，讓人感覺艱難，叫它的中文名字海蘭泡顯然更容易些。儘管海蘭泡位於西伯利亞遠東地區，但它卻充滿了歐洲風情。色彩斑斕的東正教教堂與其他歐洲風格的建築交相輝映，在夜晚發出暖色的光亮。每家餐廳都有衣帽間和禮貌的門房，這也是歐洲文化的一個體現。到達的第一天傍晚，我們走進河畔一棟新建的漂亮房子，將厚重的羽絨服遞進衣帽間。這是一家名叫「煙火燒烤」的高檔餐廳，據說處於市內最昂貴的地段。

Hovercraft toward Amur north bank / 駛向北岸的氣墊船　　　Russian architecture at night / 夜色下的俄羅斯建築

兩位中年紳士向我們走來，迎接我們的是鮑里斯・列昂尼多維奇・貝爾博羅多夫和根納季・弗拉基米羅維奇・伊拉里奧諾夫。要清楚地記得城市的名字已經夠難了，這些人的名字更是讓人絕望。他們兩位都是居住在西伯利亞的俄羅斯人，這裡我指的俄羅斯人是東斯拉夫的一個族群。但在遠東地區遇到一位有著亞洲面孔的俄羅斯籍並不稀奇，我們年輕的翻譯兼導遊麥克就是這樣一位來自極地城市雅庫茨克的亞洲面孔。我非常感激他，因為他有一個簡短又好記的姓氏——伊萬諾夫，畢竟接下來的兩週我們將與他形影不離。麥克畢業於俄羅斯排名第一的莫斯科國立大學的哲學系，他曾廣泛遊歷過歐洲和亞洲，是一位博學多識且彬彬有禮的年輕人。

鮑里斯是俄中友好協會的主席，根納季是俄羅斯地理學會阿穆爾州分會的主席。前者是一個在這個邊境城市新成立的組織，而俄羅斯地理學會則早在一八四五年沙俄時期就成立了，當時叫做俄羅斯帝國地理學會。後來，前綴改成了「蘇聯」，後又變成「俄羅斯」，只不過帝國早已不見，學會主

Street of Siberia / 西伯利亞的街道
HM in snow & ice / HM 在冰雪世界

席非一般常人或學者——普京。晚餐前，鮑里斯向我們展示了一部描繪西伯利亞自然美景的影片，片中有許多由無人機拍攝的空中景象，絕大部分是夏天拍攝的，估計是因為冬天只能看見茫茫一片雪白。晚餐非常豐盛，牛排、烤魚還有美味的香腸，最開心的是我第一次品嘗到了正宗的俄式羅宋湯。我本來還擔心桌上出現一些我消受不得的高濃度伏特加，畢竟印象裡這是北極地區的餐桌上最常見的飲品，還好兩位主人貼心地為我們準備一些上好的葡萄酒，整餐下來我可謂大飽口福。

不知什麼原因，我們六人小隊到訪的消息似乎在這個小城傳開了。看來即使網路上中國探險學會和我個人的資料寥寥無幾，但已足以在這個遙遠的角落為我們打開一扇友好交流的大門。他們甚至知道最新的消息：香港大學剛剛成立了一個以我的名字命名的探險中心。因此，我們並沒有被當作普通遊客對待，接待禮遇比預期的更加正式。

意料之外地，接下來幾天的行程被重新安排得滿滿當當。簡要參觀完斯沃博德內自然公園後，我將被邀請去當地的阿穆爾州立大學進行參觀和客座演講。在那之後，還有在州立科學圖書館的一場電視採訪和公開講座。所有的安排都變得即興起來，要知道，以往我甚至會提前一個月規劃和準備講座或採訪。我不禁想到，或許是因為當前國際社會對俄羅斯的制裁，才讓來自中國的我們更加被重視。經濟制裁帶來的影響體現在方方面面的細節上，比如我最愛的可口可樂撤離了俄羅斯，現在在這只能喝到它的各類替代品，味道和外觀都還算差強人意。還有我平時每週都要吃一次的麥當勞，在這只能找到它的「倒版」，一些餐廳把金拱門的標誌倒掛，同樣賣快餐，還被一江之隔黑河市內的某些商家模仿。

鑒於我對西伯利亞的了解太少，實在無法自己規劃穿越邊境的行程，所以只能拜託我們的嚮導。我提出的唯一要求是，我們不是遊客，也不打算成為遊客。一直以來，我習慣了獨立規劃團隊的行程，所以這次不可避免地感覺自己像是被某位俄羅斯象棋大師操控的棋子，被隆重對待，但也被期待有所表現。當聽說在接近零下三十度的黑龍江上冰釣也是行程的一環時，我開始有點擔心下一場遊戲會不會是危險的俄羅斯手槍輪盤了。但他們的溫暖和善意令我不自覺地安心，所以也就順其自然，聽從他們的安排了。

在海蘭泡的第二天，我們幾乎花了一整天時間，在冰天雪地中驅車前往約一百五十公里外的遙遠小鎮——斯沃博德內。這個小鎮很有邊疆風格，許多木製農舍錯落有致，但其實它曾經是一個主要的古拉格社區。十九世紀末到二十世紀初，西伯利亞大鐵路修建期間，有超過二十萬流放者在這裡進行強制勞動。如今，它的居民數量只有當年的四分之一。參觀一個被大雪覆蓋的植物園對我來說還是頭一回。我盡職地在高大的松樹和冷杉林中轉了一

Svobodny Arboretum / 斯沃博德尼植物園
Eurasian Red Squirrel morph / 歐亞紅松鼠的變種

圈，心裡念著這可別是在為之後更強烈的冰雪活動熱身。這個植物園實際上是一個森林科學實驗站，由俄羅斯博物學家伊萬‧密丘林創建，入口處有他的半身雕像。據說，他培育了三百多種新的漿果和水果品種。雖然沒有看到著名的西伯利亞飛鼠，但我遇見了耳朵上有絨毛的小松鼠，牠看起來跟美國西南部的纓耳松鼠一模一樣，恍惚間我以為這個物種從新世界移民到了舊世界。實際上，牠是歐亞紅松鼠的深色變種，我注意到了牠耳朵上方的紅色絨毛。

在回程的路上，我們在路邊遇到了一個支在拖車上的漂亮小攤，攤主奧列西婭在賣自製的果酒和從黑龍江裡剛捕到的狗魚。我花了八百盧布，約合九美元，買了一條半米長的狗魚。由於沒有地方煮這魚，最後牠隨著我們的中國晚餐一起回了鮑里斯家。

事情是這樣的，為了回報鮑里斯和根納季兩位主席的好意，第二天晚上我們想作東，請他們吃一頓中國菜。鎮上最好的中餐廳據說是一家火鍋店，於是我們徑直去了那裡，它開在一個新開業的商場裡，門口有兩盞紅彤彤的中式燈籠。還好我們有提前預訂，那家餐廳相當熱門，坐滿了當地的俄羅斯人。菜單上有糖醋里肌等典型的中餐，但重頭戲肯定還是我們自帶的魚。我走向櫃檯，想跟廚師交代一下怎麼做我們那條魚，結果尷尬地發現，這裡不光所有的服務員都是俄羅斯人，就連廚師和店長也是，我們根本沒法溝通，他也理所當然地婉拒了我們做魚的請求。所以到最後，我們只能把那條凍得硬邦邦的魚整個送給鮑里斯了。

翌日大清早，阿穆爾州立大學國際商務系主任瓦倫蒂娜就已經站在校門口迎接我們了。她帶我們參觀了幾棟教學樓後，來到一間大教室，裡面已有五六十名學生靜靜地坐著。

這些大都是中文系一年級的學生，中文水平還不夠熟練，所以我用英語演講，再由我們的導遊麥克做即時翻譯。講座本身的內容比較常規，學會的電影也一如既往的能引起大家的情感共鳴，但在演講結束後，我突然覺得有一束強光打在我的身上，感覺瞬間變成了超級明星一樣，因為這些學生和老師們紛紛湧到前面拿著筆記本來找我要簽名，有的還要合照。霎時間，我比滔滔不絕地演講時還要忙得不可開交。

當天下午，我被帶到州立科學圖書館，進行了一場十五分鐘的電視採訪。全俄國家電視廣播公司下屬的新聞頻道「俄羅斯二十四」的主播達娜・切爾尼雪娃問了一些有趣的問題，她尤其感興趣的是

Young members of RAS / 俄羅斯地理學會的年輕成員

我和我的團隊多年來對幾個亞洲境內江河源頭的探索經歷。我實話對她說，其實我來西伯利亞的主要目的就是要探索這裡的兩條河流。第一是勒拿河，它從貝加爾湖流入北冰洋，是世界上第十一長的河流。另一條就是目前我們所能看到的這條阿穆爾河，也就是黑龍江，這條河界定了中國和俄羅斯的國界。我猜這個採訪當晚就播出了，因為第二天我們就收到了節目的連結。關於我們到訪的新聞報導也在兩天之內被發布在俄羅斯地理學會的網站上，足以見得俄羅斯人的辦事效率有多高。

採訪結束後，我被帶到另一間講堂，裡面坐著大約八十人，看起來都是中年以上的年紀。他們是俄羅斯地理學會的成員，其中大約只有二十個年輕人，女性似乎比男性多出四倍。

從聽眾的熱烈反響來看，講座應該很受歡迎。提問的人一個接著一個，結束後大家也是跟上午一樣，熱情地湧到前面來拍照。不過我不得不盡快趕去火車站，乘坐過夜火車前往下一個目的地，前面還有更多精彩的活動等著我們。

火車在黑暗中駛出車站，車輪的節奏聲讓我想起了熟悉的〈伏爾加船夫曲〉，獨唱深沉，合唱震撼。忽然，我的眼前浮現出了一群勇敢者的身影，那是開闢了這條道路的人們，我不禁想，他們到底經歷了多少艱辛，克服了多少困難，才將這鐵路從歐洲延伸至遠東的海岸。窗外大雪紛飛，而車廂溫暖，我窩在臥鋪中漸漸入睡，心中充滿了對這些堅韌不拔的人民的敬意。此刻，政治彷彿只是落在浩瀚書卷上的一粒塵埃，隨手一撫，便了無蹤跡。

Russian Geographical Society / 來自俄羅斯地理學會的觀眾
Russian TV interview / 俄羅斯電視採訪

踏雪披霜的西伯利亞奇行錄　第二章

WINTER EXPEDITION TO SIBERIA (Part 2)

Siberia Far East – Nov 26 to Dec 7, 2023

WINTER EXPEDITION TO SIBERIA (Part 2)
Ice fishing on the Amur and more

The fish is still jumping and flapping its tail as I pull my line up from the ice hole. But within a minute, even before I am able to take the hook off, it is frozen stiff. The water below some twelve or more inches of ice must feel warm, being above zero. The frozen ice, barely below freezing at its equilibrium, becomes the flowing river's blanket for insulation. Whereas the air temperature around me above the Amur River is at most minus twenty, windchill not factored in. It really doesn't matter how low exactly. As I always say, anything below minus twenty is irrelevant. Numb is numb, you won't feel the difference. Perhaps I should extrapolate; dead is dead, you won't know your legacy. It may, however, be a model for the living.

Amur River is for the Chinese the Black Dragon, the Heilongjiang, that long river that defines the border of Russia and China before flowing north to enter the sea near the tip of the island of Sakhalin. Here, I am surrounded by a sea of white in the Russian Far East, Siberia that is. Snow, so very pure and pristine, is like cosmetic makeup on a woman, covering all the unwanted blemishes. I look around and say it quietly to Mikhail, our young Russian interpreter/guide, making sure our three lady team members are out of listening distance.

Numbing recreation / 會把人凍僵的消遣　　　　　　　　Fish caught in ice / 冰中釣魚

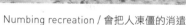

I have observed ice fishing since my college days, first around the St Croix River bordering Wisconsin and Minnesota. Then in the 1980s, while on expedition for the National Geographic documenting the Ewenki tribe just south of the border with the Soviet Union, and again more recently during my annual winter excursions to eastern Hokkaido for wildlife viewing and bird watching. But this is the first time I actually tried my hand at it, though briefly. We are still more than three weeks away from winter solstice and the sun sets at 4pm, so far north in latitude are we. What also amazes me is related to the longitude. When in tropical or subtropical latitudes, you fly a few hours before switching your watch forward or backward in time. High up towards the arctic, a few hours drive may cross one time zone, since the longitude lines become closer and closer to each other as the globe narrows, before joining at the poles.

Here living along the bank of the Amur River is Albert Babaev. Albert is an elderly gentleman of around 60 who operates a hunting/fishing outfit called Sarapuskya Atmosphera. A huge dome building shows that this is a rather

Flag, ladder & crossbows / 旗幟、梯子和弩弓

modern homestay with many rooms behind the dome for accommodation. Inside, a spacious kitchen with projector and screen above the dining table shows that this is a multi-purpose room. An aluminum ladder leads to a loft above, overhung with several large flags, that of Russia, China, South Korea, USA and UK.

Apparently, Albert has hosted multinationals to his hunting and fishing abode, mainly during the short summer, as evidenced by the many photos he put up on his wall of guests angling huge fish out of the Amur. There were even two Remington crossbows hung on the ladder stairs. I offer him our newly made flag of the University of Hong Kong Wong How Man Centre for Exploration to add on.

Winter is brutal here. There is no cold front, as Siberia is the home of such fronts, with the temperature falling to forty below as the norm rather than exception. Today the temperature is lingering just south of thirty degrees below freezing. Albert soon asks us to put back on our heavy coats to go out of the warm house. Ahead sits a double seat snowmobile with two sleds towed behind. Albert is like a modern Santa going out into the snow in his sleds. We scramble into the sleds and cover ourselves with heavy blankets and thick leather overcoats over our body and legs. As white steamy clouds blow out of the exhaust pipe, we are pulled through the thick snow and *down the bank onto the frozen river with the chilling wind cutting into our faces like a knife.*

Some four hundred meters away, I can see small dots of tents and a few cars parked on the ice. This is our next destination. When the snowmobile stops, Albert ushers us into a sizable tent sitting on the open ice. There is a table set up and two small gas stoves providing minimal heat to nurse our red frozen faces. Hot tea is served in metal cups that become our handwarmers.

Once we warm up a bit, Albert leads us out some fifty meters away to observe two older gentlemen sitting behind a makeshift fence while fishing out of a hole drilled through the thick ice. One man gave me a big welcoming smile and I can see that gold teeth is still popular ornaments this far north. Peeking through the hole, it seems the ice at this moment and this place is around half a meter thick, obviously enough for a car to drive on top, as several are parked nearby. There is a big bag on the ground and looking in, I find three large and frozen pike inside. These are the most prevalent fish on the Amur River. Each measures almost a meter long and must weigh around four to five kilos.

Sled & tent / 雪橇和帳篷

Team smokers / 吸煙者

With a power drill, a fishing hole is opened and a chair put next to it for us to try our luck. I sit there momentarily but soon lose patience in the cold. While I am inside the tent sipping tea, there is a commotion outside, as Albert has just pulled up another pike. I quickly go out and take hold of the line with the fish still jumping and flapping for my photo op and bragging rights to irritate all my fishing friends. Within a couple minutes, the fish is frozen stiff, as if coming out of a fish monger's freezer.

Factoring in windchill, the weather is too brutal for an extended stay. So, after an hour or so of outing, we opt to head back to Albert's home for lunch. Coming in from the cold, his home-cooked bortsch soup somehow tastes more authentic even than the one I had two days ago in a Russian restaurant, whether real or imagined. Albert also shows us his collection of early rock carvings from the area and gives us some smaller replica pieces as souvenirs. He

HM icefishing / HM 在冰釣

Amur River icefishing spot / 阿穆爾河上的冰釣點
Catch in the summer / 夏日漁獲

says he is very fond of Hong Kong, having visited it several times, including even a prospectus business meeting at the HSBC headquarters building.

He also knows China well, as can be seen from his bookshelf, with a rare book about the 88th Separate Rifle Brigade. That was a Chinese and Korean guerilla unit that was integrated into the Soviet Red Army in 1942 to fight against the Japanese along the northeastern frontiers during WWII.

Kim Il Sung who founded North Korea was Captain of a Korean battalion serving alongside Chinese commanders. Rumors have it that Kim Jong Il was born in the village near here. The brigade was stationed along the bank of the Amur River around seventy-five kilometers north of the city of Khabarovsk at Vyatskoye Village, near where we are now. The village, along with Khabarovsk and Vladivostok, was ceded to Imperial Russia by the Qing Dynasty as part of Russian Manchuria in the 1860 Convention of Peking.

Our hour-and-a-half drive from Khabarovsk to Vyatskoye is worth recounting, now over a snow-covered paved road. Alexander is a rather common Russian name. But this Alexander sitting next to me in the driver's seat is also Speedy Gonzales and Yosemite Sam, characters from the Bugs Bunny comic, all rolled into one. Diminutive in build for a Russian, he drives with his foot pressing the accelerator to the floor, looking perfectly at ease while passing car after car on the snow as the speedometer hits well over 100. And we are seven of us in our team, crammed into an eight-passenger van with all our luggage.

Yosemite Sam carries one long-barrel revolver in each hand, firing off at will. Alex is also busy with both hands, not so much on the steering wheel. In between fiddling with his mobile phone searching over the map for our hidden destination, his right hand is busy picking out of a box of sunflower seeds. Like clockwork, he passes the seed to his left hand, proceeds to put it in his mouth and, with a small cracking sound, sucks out the seed and spits out the shell, again into his left hand to put into another box by his car's door. This action continues for the entire time of our drive for the next hour and a half over a road cutting through a thick wilderness forest of white-barked leafless birch and snow-clad evergreen fir and spruce.

The chill of a Siberian winter plus the thrill of Alex's driving must have intoxicated my frozen senses. I unstrap my seatbelt and release myself from the tight hold of two layers of down jackets and additional underclothing. This momentary freedom will cost me 1000 Rubles (equivalent to US$13), as a freeway camera picks up my image in the front seat without seat belt on. A very fine image with a figure of the fine to be paid is quickly sent to Alex's mobile phone soon after.

Russian Roullet has got me in its crosshair. But the thrill of a gambler's chance at the risk of skidding and hitting the snow-bank is paid off only in a small monetary loss. I return to Khabarovsk safe and sound, and in one piece, but with a light heart and a slightly lightened wallet.

踏雪披霜的西伯利亞奇行錄 第二章 冰釣奇緣

當我從冰洞裡拉起釣線時，魚還在鮮活地跳動，不停地拍打尾巴。但不到一分鐘後，甚至我還沒來得及把魚鉤取下，牠就已經凍僵了。冰層下約十二英寸以上的水，溫度才能達到零度以上。而冰層本身就像是流動河水的保溫毯，僅僅在冰點以下，冷得刺骨。冰面之上，我的周圍，空氣溫度最高是零下二十度，像刀子一樣的風刮過來的時候，體感溫度可還要低得多。不過實際溫度到底有多低其實已經不重要了。我常說，零下二十度以下的溫度都是一樣的。麻木就是麻木，你不會感覺有什麼區別。就像死亡就是死亡，你不會知道你給活著的人留下了什麼，痛苦、遺憾、開心、慶幸、難過，這些情緒都與你無關了，感受不到，也沒機會在意。

對中國人而言，阿穆爾河就是黑龍江。這條界定了俄羅斯和中國邊界的河流奔騰不息，向北流入靠近庫頁島尖端的鄂霍次克海。哆哆嗦嗦地站在冰面上的我再次有種被白色海洋包圍的感覺，不禁感嘆，這就是西伯利亞。所謂「一白遮百醜」，純淨無瑕的雪，就像女人的化妝品，掩蓋了所有你不想要的瑕疵。我環顧四周，悄悄地對我們年輕的導遊麥克說，可千萬別讓我們的三位女隊員聽到。

從大學時代起，我就淺淺接觸過冰釣。最初是在威斯康辛州和明尼蘇達州交界的聖克羅伊河一帶。八十年代，我為美國《國家地理雜誌》記錄蘇聯邊境南邊的鄂溫克族時，也見過當地人冰釣。最近幾年，我每年冬天都會去北海道東部觀鳥，在那裡也有人冰釣。雖然時間很短，但這次是我第一次真的下手，親自嘗試冰釣。我們現在離冬至還有三個多星期，然而因為緯度太北，太陽下午四點就落山了。讓我感到驚奇的還有經度的變化。在靠近北極的這裡，開車幾小時就可能跨過一個時區，然而在熱帶或亞熱帶地區，只有跨過飛行數小時的距離後，才需要調整手錶的時間。原理我明白，是因為經度線在赤道上最遠，越靠近兩極距離越小，最後會在極點匯合。但只有親身到了極地，才會有這種時間混亂的真實感。

阿爾伯特・巴巴耶夫今年大約六十歲，他在阿穆爾河岸邊經營著一家名為大氣層的狩獵加釣魚營地，裡面還有許多房間提供住宿。他的營地相當現代化，巨大的圓頂主建築內有一個寬敞的廚房，餐桌上方有投影機和螢幕，旁邊放著蘇聯時期的書。一架鋁製梯子通往上面的閣樓，閣樓上掛著各種旗幟，包括俄羅斯、中國、韓國、美國和英國的國旗，應該是他的主要客源。

結合他的照片牆也不難看出，阿爾伯特在短暫的夏季接待過來自多國的客人。照片中的客人們興奮地捧著戰利品，阿穆爾河中的魚大得嚇人。梯子旁邊還掛著兩把雷明頓十字弓，他說是客人送給他的紀念品。聽完，我也送給他一個特別的紀念品——一面香港大學黃效文探險中心的新旗幟，上面有我的簽名。他開心地收

HM's catch / HM 的收穫

Domed CERS team / CERS 團隊合影
Feasting on fish caught / 漁獲美食

下，並掛到了那面通往閣樓的牆上，並如一面國旗。

我不得不用冷酷無情來形容這裡的冬天。沒有冷鋒的概念，因為這裡就是冷鋒本身，氣溫驟降到零下四十度是常態。今天氣溫徘徊在零下三十度左右，阿爾伯特在發放過保暖鞋墊以後，囑咐我們穿上最厚的外套，準備離開溫暖的屋子。屋前停著一台雙座雪地摩托車，後面拖著兩個雪橇。阿爾伯特活像個現代版的聖誕老人，上前駕上了他的魔法小車。我們急忙爬進雪橇，用厚重的毯子和皮外套裹住腿部。白色的蒸汽從排氣管中呼嘯而出，我們穿過厚厚的積雪，滑下河岸，進入結冰的河面。凜冽的寒風吹過，霎時間，裸露在外的臉部皮膚像要被冰針刺穿。

大約四百米外，我看到冰面上有一處小帳篷和幾輛停著的車，估計就是我們的目的地。果不其然，雪地摩托車停下，阿爾伯特帶我們進入了那個搭在冰上的帳篷。帳篷裡有一張放滿零食和茶壺的小桌子，旁邊兩個小煤氣爐散發著微弱的熱量，大家都不自覺地把凍紅的臉湊了過去。熱茶倒進金屬杯中，成了我們的暖手寶。一時間帳篷裡大家吸鼻涕的聲音此起彼伏，不吸菸的成員此刻嘴裡也冒出了「白煙」。

稍微暖和了一點後，阿爾伯特帶我們走出約五十米遠，去觀察兩位坐在臨時圍欄後釣魚的老先生。厚冰鑽出的洞口上，他們搗得

Albert & HM with flag / 阿爾伯特和 HM 與香港大學旗幟

Team on sled / 乘雪橇的 CERS 團隊

只剩一雙眼睛，靜靜坐在那裡垂釣。其中一位老先生見我們過來，給了我一個大大的微笑，嘴裡的金牙亮得反光。我不禁想，原來金牙在這麼北的地方也算流行的裝飾品，那在這樣冷的天氣裡舔一下牙，會不會把舌頭黏住呢？附近停了好幾輛轎車，透過洞口往裡看，冰層足足有半米厚，我才了然這冰面足夠承受車的重量。冰面上有個大袋子，裡面裝著三條裹著厚霜的大梭魚。梭魚是阿穆爾河中最常見的魚類，差不多有一米長，重約四到五公斤。

阿爾伯特用電鑽開了一個釣魚洞，旁邊放了把摺疊椅，讓我們試試運氣。我坐了一會兒，但很快耐不住嚴寒，只能回到帳篷裡喝茶。不久後，外面傳來一陣騷動，原來是阿爾伯特又釣到了一條大梭魚。我迅速跑出去，抓住那條還在跳動的大魚拍了個照，想著發給我的那些釣魚佬朋友們，讓他們羨慕一下。幾分鐘內，這條魚就變得硬梆梆了，像是剛從魚販的冷凍庫裡拿出來的一樣。

大約一個多小時後，考慮到大家就快凍成冰雕了，我們於是決定回到阿爾伯特家裡享用午餐。一進到溫暖的室內，他親手煮的羅宋湯的香味撲鼻而來。不知是不是心理作用，我覺得這湯竟比我兩天前在海蘭泡高級餐廳喝到的還要美味。阿爾伯特興致勃勃地向我們展示了他收藏的當地早期岩刻，並送了我們一些小型複製品作為紀念。他說他非常喜歡香港，曾多次造訪，還參加過在匯豐總部大樓裡舉行的商業會議。

阿爾伯特對中國也頗有了解，這從他書架上的書籍可以窺見。其中一本關於第八十八獨立步兵旅的珍貴書籍引起了我的注意。這是一支在二戰期間整編入蘇聯紅軍的中朝游擊隊，於一九四二年在東北前線對抗日本。

如今北韓的創立者金日成曾是這支部隊中一個朝鮮營的營長，與中國指揮官並肩作戰。這支部隊駐紮在阿穆爾河沿岸距離哈巴羅夫斯克市約七十五公里的維亞茨科耶村，也正是我們現在所在的地方。傳聞說，金正日就出生在這附近。歷史上，這片地區連同哈巴羅夫斯克和符拉迪沃斯托克一起，於一八六〇年北京條約簽訂後被清朝割讓給俄羅斯帝國，成為俄屬滿洲的一部分。

我們從哈巴羅夫斯克到維亞茨科耶村的一個半小時車程值得一提。亞歷山大這個名字在俄羅斯很常見，但坐在我旁邊駕駛座上的那位亞歷山大可不一般。他可謂是「飛毛腿岡薩雷斯」和「燥山姆」的結合體，我都要懷疑華納兄弟是以他為原型創造的這兩個動漫形象了。對於俄羅斯人來說，他的身材算是矮小的，但卻十分慓悍。開車時油門踩到底，不管不顧地在滑面雪地上超車，速度表早已超過每小時一百公里。要不是我們七個人連同所有行李擠在一輛載客八人的小巴上，我還以為他開得是什麼超速跑車。

Fisherman gold teeth / 漁夫的金牙
Digging ice hole / 挖冰洞

Alex driving habit / 駕駛習慣獨特的亞歷山大
HM shot by speed camera /
HM 被測速相機拍到

動畫裡，燥山姆雙手各持一把長槍，隨意開火。現實中亞歷山大的雙手也沒閒著，但不是忙在方向盤上。他左手用手機在地圖上搜尋我們的目的地，右手忙著從一個小盒子裡挑選葵花籽。他把瓜子傳到左手，放進嘴裡，隨著一聲輕微的破裂聲，吸出瓜子仁，吐出殼，再放進車門邊的另一個盒子裡。整套動作下來流暢得像走了上億遍的鐘錶時針，而這套動作將在接下來一個半小時的車程中不斷重複。為了不過度擔心我們的行車安全，我乾脆眼不見心不煩，把目光投向窗外。此時我們正穿過一片片白樺樹和覆蓋著積雪的常青樹林，飛雪像流螢打在車窗上，好像童話一樣的場景。

坐在亞歷山大的副駕很難不感覺壓力山大，行至後半程，我甚至在西伯利亞的冬天感覺到了一絲燥熱。於是我解開了安全帶，脫掉兩層羽絨服和厚厚的內衣，享受片刻的自由。這短暫的自由可是我花了一千盧布，合計約十三美元買回來的，因為高速公路上的攝影機拍下了我在前座未繫安全帶的照片。俄羅斯人一如既往的高效，很快，一張罰款通知單就發到了亞歷山大的手機上。

我擔心過的事終究還是發生了，俄羅斯輪盤遊戲選中了我們，並最終瞄準了我一個人。不過好在有驚無險，我們安全無虞地回到了哈巴羅夫斯克。錢包輕了些無所謂，只要心情最終輕快了，就是值得慶祝的好事。

Albert & team / 阿爾伯特和團隊

踏雪披霜的西伯利亞奇行錄　第三章

WINTER EXPEDITION TO SIBERIA (Part 3)

Siberia Far East – Nov 26 to Dec 7, 2023

WINTER EXPEDITION TO SIBERIA (Part 3)
A little-known Jewish community

The overnight train ride from Blagoveshchensk to Birobidzhan takes almost twelve hours for a distance of 420 kilometers. Today, China's fastest express train would cover that in slightly over an hour. Driving, however, would also take seven hours. We opt for the train, to match the pace of Siberia, to experience a Russian train ride, plus to save the cost of one night in a hotel. Security measures at the station are similar to those at airports. I observe a rather stylish Russian lady in mink coat joining us in line. Mink is naturally in style for such Siberian winters.

The sleeping car is similar to those of Eurail with one bunk to each side of the door. I take a peek in the dining car and find all seats are taken. I assume vodka and beer are the main course, and the food is just a side order. I buy a modestly priced bottle of wine, and stand to have a glass before retiring to my cabin. Our reservations cover two cabins, and soon I fall asleep to the sound of the tracks as well as the song and card game noise of our younger team members in the adjacent cabin.

We arrive at Birobidzhan station at 8:10 in the morning, and step off the train onto the platform in darkness with moon light. Winter sun rises late in high latitude Siberia. Greeting us inside the station is Alexander, father of our HKU student friend Vasilii. He is chapter president of the

Dining car / 餐車內部

Russian Geographical Society (RGS) in Yakutsk of northern Siberia. He has taken a flight here just to greet us personally.

The station has both Russian and Hebrew written over it – "Birobidzhan". Once outside the train station, the first sight is a tall-standing menorah, the candelabra symbol of the Jewish religion. This has come to represent this Jewish Autonomous Oblast, or Province, of Russia. I have made a special request to stop here, as this is the only government-designated Jewish community in the world, besides Israel in the Middle East. At its peak, there were a concentration of over 50,000 Russian Jews living in this community, with the early Soviet government hoping to turn the Jewish population from businessmen and craftsmen to homestead agriculturalists.

The attempt largely failed and, by the late 1980s with the relaxation of immigration policy, most of the Jews who first settled here in the 1930s had left for Israel, America or other western countries. Today less than 1,000 Jews remain in this Jewish namesake community, with the rest being Russian. They live in a province with a size exactly the same as that of Taiwan, but with only 1/200th of its population. That is not unusual for the huge land mass of Siberia.

As time is limited, we head for breakfast at the best Jewish restaurant in town. Soon a sumptuous Kosher breakfast is served by two young ladies. In the background is a mannequin of a woman dressed in traditional Jewish costume. The dishes are both colorful and tasty. A block away is the local synagogue. Valery Gurevitch is on hand to walk us through the synagogue. He is 75 years old and an honorary citizen of the Jewish Autonomous Oblast (JAO) as well as chairman of the federation of Jewish Organizations.

Downstairs in the synagogue, where maybe up to fifty can be seated, is the men's section with a

Arriving at Birobidzhan / 抵達比羅比詹

Menorah outside station / 車站外的燭台

small altar in the middle and stacks of religious books along the walls. Upstairs is a balcony where ladies can look down to observe service. By the altar is a wooden cabinet where their holy book is kept. There is also a fair-sized library of old books related to the stories and history of the Jews, including several about the Jews of Heilongjiang across the border on the China side. In a small exhibit room are a case of medals received during the Soviet era and old pictures of the JAO when the early pioneers conducted agriculture on the farm, including images showing use of old farming machines. There are also displays of old utensils and implements like an obsolete typewriter and some old texts. A gramophone, an old telephone and camera make up the remaining displays.

Valery also takes the time to explain to us some of the ceremonial objects used during religious service, including a display explaining the use of the tefillin, a tiny square box containing miniature sacred scrolls, worn on the forehead of male members during the Shabbat service. Valery speaks proudly of his heritage, saying that he has visited his relatives many times in Israel but prefers to live here where he was born and brought up, having no intention to immigrate. As we exit the synagogue, in front in the courtyard is a stone engraving in memory of

Kosher restaurant / 猶太潔食餐廳

A fine kosher meal / 美味的猶太食物

Synagogue altar & seats / 祭壇和座位
Synagogue at JAO / 猶太教堂

Bird diversity at Bastak / 巴斯塔克的鳥類多樣性
Mammal diversity at Bastak /
巴斯塔克的哺乳動物多樣性

Jews killed by the Nazis between 1933 to 1945, tragic crimes that should never be forgotten. Perhaps someday similar monuments will be erected at Wounded Knee, in the Banda Spice Islands, in Nanjing, and even Gaza... despite controversy of a few with selective memory and dual standards.

The two women, Anna Zubareva and Katya, become our guides. Anna is the president of the newly formed local chapter of the Russian Geographical Society. Katya is an expert researcher on forest fire, and she takes us on a visit to the Bastak State Nature Reserve. We hike along a frozen stream and up and down a hill through deep snow where sign boards explain the flora and fauna of the region. The most distinguished among the fauna is the Amur Tiger. These rare tigers, highly endangered, are also known as the Siberian or Manchurian tigers. Only less than 400 such animals exist in Siberia with some living in this border reserve by the Amur River. On the China side, there are less than 50 in the wild. Since the tiger can cross the border Amur River freely, over frozen ice in the winter or even swim across during the summer, I suppose they are the most welcome illegal immigrant across the international border even without a visa.

At the end of the hike, we are served hot tea in an outdoor kiosk, though we try to finish our beverage quickly in order to return into the warmth of our waiting car. A Siberian winter is not ideal for an extended outdoor hike.

Soon we are to leave for a three-hour car ride to Khabarovsk, another city also along the left bank of the Amur River on the border with China. From there, we will catch a flight to the largest island of Russia – Sakhalin. It is by the coast of Russia and, at its closest, only forty kilometers from Hokkaido in Japan where I have spent many wonderful winters photographing wildlife, especially the Red-crowned Crane. This is another rare species that crosses the international border without permit. Politically sanctioned or not, it remains a most welcome guest to Russia, Japan, China, even to both of the two Koreas. In many cases, animals today enjoy more freedom than us humans, even during the coldest months in Siberia.

Hot tea at cold kiosk / 寒冷小亭子裡的熱茶

踏雪披霜的西伯利亞奇行錄 第三章　鮮為人知的猶太社區

從布拉戈維申斯克到比羅比詹的夜班火車，行駛時間近十二個小時，路程約四百二十公里。而在如今的中國，同樣的距離，高鐵最快只需一個多小時就能跑完。開車的話，也得花上七個小時。最終我們選擇了火車，既能配合西伯利亞的節奏，又能體驗一下俄羅斯的雪國列車，還能省下一晚住酒店的費用，一舉三得。車站的安檢措施和機場差不多，排隊的時候我瞥見一位穿著貂皮大衣的俄羅斯女士，相當時髦，果然貂皮與西伯利亞天生相配。

軟臥車廂和歐洲的火車臥鋪很相似，每扇門兩邊各有一張上下鋪床。我溜達到餐車，發現所有座位都已經坐滿了，只不過伏特加和啤酒才是主角，食物只是配角。我還是承受不了伏特加的強烈，買了一瓶價格實惠的葡萄酒，站著小酌一杯後回到我們包廂。不久後，便在鐵軌咔嗒咔嗒的節奏聲和隔壁包廂年輕隊員們的戲鬧聲中安然入睡。

我們在次日早上八點十分抵達比羅比詹火車站。邁出車廂的那一刻，月光下的站台依舊籠罩在黑暗中。高緯度的西伯利亞冬季，日出總是姍姍來遲。在站內迎接我們的是亞歷山大，他是我們香港大學的朋友瓦西里的父親，也是俄羅斯地理學會在北西伯利亞雅庫茨克分會的會長。他昨夜特意搭飛機從雅庫茨克趕來，只為了親自迎接我們。

車站上方，醒目的俄文和希伯來文的「比羅比詹」字樣並排而立。走出車站，首先映入眼簾的是一座高高矗立的猶太教燭台，它是這個猶太自治州的象徵。先前規劃行程時，我特意要求在此停留，因為這是世界上除以色列之外，唯一一個由政府指定的猶太社區。在它的鼎盛時期，曾聚集著超過五萬名俄羅斯籍猶太人。早期的蘇聯政府曾希望透過建立發展這個社區，將猶太人從商人和工匠轉變為自給自足的農民。

這個嘗試最終並未成功，到一九八〇年代末，隨著移民政策的放寬，最初在一九三〇年代定居於此的猶太人多數已經前往以色列、美國或其他西方國家。如今，這個曾經的猶太社區，猶太裔已不到一千人，其餘的居民大多是俄羅斯人。他們生活在一片面積與台灣相同的土地，但人口卻只有台灣的二百分之一。不過此般人口密度在地廣人稀的西伯利亞大地上也並不罕見。

由於時間緊迫，我們直奔鎮上最負盛名的猶太餐廳享用早餐。不一會兒，兩位年輕的女服務生就端上了一桌豐盛的猶太潔食早餐。背景中，有一個身著傳統猶太服飾的女性人偶端著菜，帶著歡迎的笑容。餐桌上的菜餚色彩繽紛，每一道都散發著獨特的風味。離餐廳約一個街口的距離有一個猶太教堂。瓦列里·古列維奇在那裡等著帶我們參觀，他今年七十五歲，是猶太自治州的榮譽市民，也是當地猶太組織聯合會的主席。

HM in train cabin / 在火車車廂裡的 HM
Street of Birobidzhan / 比羅比詹街頭

Stylish Russian in mink /
穿著時髦貂皮大衣的俄羅斯女士

這間猶太教堂分上下兩層，下層是可容納約五十位男士的區域，中央有一個小祭壇，四周堆滿了宗教書籍，旁邊有一個木製櫥櫃，裡面保存著他們的聖書。樓上有一個陽臺，女士們可以在這裡瞰整個教堂和儀式活動。教堂裡還有一個規模不小的圖書館，收藏著許多與猶太人歷史有關的古書。其中有幾本中文書尤為乍眼，它們講述的是居住在邊境另一側的中國猶太人的故事，其中大多數在黑龍江省。在圖書館旁邊的一間小展覽室裡，陳列著蘇聯時期獲得的勳章，以及猶太自治州早期拓荒者在農場從事農業活動的老照片。照片中清晰呈現了當時農業機械的使用場景。展覽中的實物部分還包括一些舊的器具和工具，如一臺過時的打字機和一些古老的手帳。在展室的角落裡，留聲機、老電話和一架老相機構成了一個獨特的小天地，讓我彷彿瞬間穿越回上個世紀。

瓦列里特意花時間向我們介紹了一些宗教儀式中的祭祀物品，尤其詳細解釋了「經文護符匣」的用法。這是一個黑色的小方皮匣，裡面裝有微型的經文卷軸。在安息日儀式期間，男性會將這個盒子戴在額頭上。瓦列里談起他的傳統和文化時總是十分自豪，他說他疫情前曾多次前往以色列探望親戚，但從沒有移民的打算。因為這裡是他土生土長的地方，他更喜歡生活在這裡。走出教堂，前院裡立著的一塊石碑清晰可見，上面刻著紀念一九三三至一九四五年間被納粹殺害的猶太人的銘文。罪行不應被遺忘，靈魂值得永遠銘記。或許有一天，在傷膝河、班達群島、南京，甚

Centre piece scripture / 中央經文
Old equipment / 舊設備

至加沙，也會豎起類似的紀念碑。人類社會裡的選擇性記憶和雙重標準會永遠存在，但過去真切發生過的事也是永遠無法被抹煞的。歷史的真相是長鳴的警鐘，將持續不斷地發出震耳欲聾的聲音。

離開教堂後，我們驅車去參觀巴斯塔克國家自然保護區。在這裡，我們的導遊是兩位女士，安娜·祖巴列娃和卡佳。安娜是俄羅斯地理學會新成立的猶太自治州分會的會長，卡佳是一位森林火災研究專家。我們沿著凍結的小溪徒步穿行，翻越積雪深厚的山丘，看著沿途的告示牌介紹這個地區的動植物群。在這些動物中，最引我注目的是阿穆爾虎。這些珍稀的老虎，也被稱作西伯利亞虎或滿洲虎，屬於極度瀕危物種。目前西伯利亞僅存不到四百隻，部分生活在阿穆爾河邊的保護區。在中國境內，野生的阿穆爾虎更是少於五十隻。不過有趣的是，牠們可以自由穿越阿穆爾河邊界。夏季靠游泳，冬季河面結冰，牠們就直接走過去對岸。我想牠們大概是最受歡迎的「非法移民」了，橫穿兩國旅行，沒有簽證也完全不是問題。

事實證明，西伯利亞的冬天並不適合長時間的戶外遠足。徒步快

Books on Chinese Jews in library / 圖書館裡關於中國猶太人的書籍
Box tefillin with scrolls / 經匣和經文卷軸
Monument of Jews killed / 猶太人大屠殺紀念碑

接近結尾時，兩位嚮導邀請我們坐在一個戶外小亭子裡享用熱茶。雖然沖茶的水是阿穆爾河的河水，奶茶也很好喝，但我們當時的唯一念想就是趕緊喝完，回車上暖和一下。

接下來，我們將乘車前往哈巴羅夫斯克，這座城市同樣位於阿穆爾河左岸，與中國接壤。從那裡，我們將搭乘飛機前往俄羅斯最大的島嶼——庫頁島。庫頁島靠近俄羅斯海岸，距離日本北海道最近處僅有四十公里。我曾在北海道度過許多美好的冬季，拍攝野生動物，觀鳥，尤其是丹頂鶴，牠也是一種不用許可就能跨越國界的珍稀物種。無論政治環境如何，牠始終是俄羅斯、日本、中國，甚至南北韓都歡迎的貴客。這樣看來，今時今日，即便是在西伯利亞最寒冷的月分裡，動物也比我們人類享有更多的自由。

CERS team at Bastak / CERS 團隊在巴斯塔克

踏雪披霜的西伯利亞奇行錄 第四章

WINTER EXPEDITION TO SIBERIA (Part 4)

Sakhalin, Siberia Far East – Nov 26 to Dec 7, 2023

улица
Колхозная 190

WINTER EXPEDITION TO SIBERIA (Part 4)
Largest island of Russia

Sakhalin is the largest island of Russia. The loss of Sakhalin, a tribute territory including much of Siberia Far East of the Qing Empire, in 1860 by treaty to Imperial Russia was a long time ago. Then the Soviet Union took charge following the fall of the Czar, until today Russia inherited this large island in Siberia Far East. In between, there was a time when the island was split in the middle, the upper half to the Czar and lower half to Japan at the end of the Russo-Japanese War in 1905. Japan gave that up in 1945 after end of WWII.

Political fortune of the island shifted as the spheres of military prowess changed over time. Historical claims are only a footnote or an appendix to muscle power. Pump up your muscle with steroid if you want interpretation rights to political claims, even dictate of international law behind a veil. Law of the jungle prevails, no matter how beautiful we package it with cosmetic to look otherwise.

For me however, Siberia and Sakhalin are both geographical names, to learn from and explore if possible. Whoever is administering it at the time, I would abide to law and order of that moment. Our flight from Khabarovsk to Yuzhno in Sakhalin took off at 8am when the sky was barely lit over the horizon from a Siberian winter. The overnight snow and ice on the plane called for de-icing in spraying by long-armed machine using alcohol to defrost the airplane's wings. The flight was barely two hours but time zone changed was one hour, as we are way north in latitude.

The very long island of Sakhalin is almost 1000 kilometers in length and about twice the size of Taiwan, yet with a population of less than half a million, compared to over thirty million in Taiwan. Might as well be, given the bitter cold would prohibit anyone except the hardiest or those sent there in exile. Resources however are plenty, from natural gas to oil to timber and coal, marine product, etc. much of which are exported to China. Japan has been cut out of being beneficiary of such resources after joining the West in sanctions of Russia after start of the Ukraine War, a political winter on top of a Siberian winter, in order to march to the same drummer. Rhetoric's apart, my journey is an eyeopener for me.

Greeting us at the airport is Gaponenko Vitaliy, a retired geography-history teacher. He would be our guide, as arranged by the Russian Geographical Society. Our first stop is a museum, attached to the former house where Anton Chekhov, noted Russian literary great, stayed while living in Sakhalin in the year 1890. He witnessed much on Sakhalin that shocked him, including floggings and forced prostitution of women. "There

Approaching Sakhalin / 靠近庫頁島
Sakhalin Airport / 薩哈林機場

were times I felt that I saw before me the extreme limits of man's degradation", he wrote. As a medical doctor, and later a seminal playwright, he described the squalid conditions the exile had to live under. His writing led to overhaul of the penal system in Siberia to becoming more humane. The museum exhibit used his description to re-enact displays of the horrid state of such people during that era, besides some early photos and featuring of early settlers and their livelihood in this frontier land.

Anasteysha is the young lady guide who moved to Sakhalin with her mother from Croatia. She walked us through the exhibits, both about intrepid early pioneers as well as the grim history of the past. Young school kids were also touring the exhibits with their teachers and were settling down in a work room to do their exercise while enjoying their box lunch. Like many of the more fortunate places in the world, children are often happy and pleasant, a huge contrast to more destitute regions and war-zone images of children we see only too often these days on the internet.

Anasteysha at museum / 博物館嚮導安娜賽蒂莎 　　　Early community photo / 早期島上社群　Display of early settlers / 早期定居者展示

I asked to visit the local fish market, as Sakhalin is famous for marine products, sold across the strait to the Hokkaido market at fraction of the price, maybe up to a quarter, in Japan, that is before sanction put a stop to it. A three-kilo King Crab may cost only between 5000 to 6500 Russian Ruble, or equivalent of 55 to 70 USD. From the southern tip of Sakhalin, Hokkaido is only forty kilometers away across the strait and can be visible on a clear day.

In the market, there are a few vendors of Asian descent selling seafood in their respective stalls. These descendants of former Korean and Japanese settlers are now a new generation of Russian-Asian who no longer speak their native language anymore, except a few short phrases for daily use. Much of the seafood are cooked and put in freezers, and we did not hesitate to purchase a huge king crab to take back to our hotel as snack during our own Happy Hour.

Vitaliy has in his small knapsack several scrap books that he brought out from time to time to show me proudly. Apparently, these are used for his teaching, on the geography and history of Sakhalin. They are images of

Early lighthouse / 早期燈塔
Early settlers / 早期定居者
Kids at museum / 博物館裡的孩子們

Faces of Sakhalin / 來自庫頁島臉龐

newspaper or magazine cuttings, or copied from books. I took particular interest in his album on the Ainu, with a glimpse into these indigenous people to both Sakhalin and Hokkaido. Geographically, old images of lighthouses that guided the early maritime shipping also fascinated me. On nature, images he took of Tyuleny island in the Sea of Okhotsk tickled my urge to visit it someday. Its coastline is filled with fur seal and sea lion. During certain season the precipitous cliff side is crowded with huge colony of guillemots, in black and white dots.

Over the four days we were to spend in Sakhalin, we visited both the western coast of Nevelsk and the eastern harbor town of Kholmsk. At Kholmsk, we saw old ruins of structures and even military installations put up by the former Japanese occupiers. At both the north and south parts of Korsakov Port, there stand a monument marking the Japanese landing spot during WWII. Along the way, we stopped for a meal and tea at a hillside resort above the ocean, a Geo cupola camping style accommodations of the most modern design. It was just opened in 2023.

Wrapping up our stay at Sakhalin, I chose to visit the Orthodox church in Sakhalinsk. The grandiose of the interior and observing a few devotees quietly praying closes my short journey to this distant island of Russian Far East, before taking a flight to Vladivostok.

Orthodox church, Nevelskoye, Southwest Sakalin / 東正教堂，薩哈林西南部港口涅韋爾斯克

踏雪披霜的西伯利亞奇行錄 第四章 庫頁島的前世今生

薩哈林島，華人慣稱庫頁島，是目前俄羅斯聯邦內最大的島嶼，不過早在一八六〇年，也就是清政府與沙皇俄國簽訂臭名昭著的《北京條約》之前，這座島嶼就已經處在日俄爭奪的漩渦之中了。一九〇五年日俄戰爭結束時，根據《樸茨茅斯條約》，其北半部歸沙俄，南半部歸日本。後面隨著沙皇的垮台，蘇聯接管了這座島嶼。在二戰結束後一九四五年，日本才算澈底放棄了這片土地。今天，俄羅斯繼承了這片西伯利亞遙遠東部的巨大寶地。

一片土地的政治命運不過風中之燭，總是隨著軍事力量的變遷而起伏。歷史上的主權聲索，只不過是國家實力的註腳或附錄。一個國家，或者說一個政府，若想獲得政治主張的解釋權，甚至在幕後對國際法有操作空間，就得像健美運動員一樣，用各種類固醇來增強「肌肉」。無論我們如何精心包裝和注解人類文明，叢林法則依然是這個世界最真實的運行規則。

不過對我來說，庫頁島和西伯利亞一樣，都只是個地理名稱，我更願意深究的是它們的本質。無論土地當時由誰管轄，我都會遵守當地的法律和秩序，因為它們是值得學習和探索的土地。我們從哈巴羅夫斯克飛往庫頁島的航班起飛時間是早上八點，彼時西伯利亞冬日的天際剛剛泛起一絲微光。機翼上覆蓋了一夜的冰雪，需要長臂機用酒精噴灑除冰。雖然飛行時間不到兩小時，但由於我們位於緯度較高的地方，時區變化了一小時。

狹長的庫頁島幾乎有一千公里長，面積約為台灣的兩倍，但人口卻不到五十萬，而台灣則超過三千萬。這也不難理解，畢竟這兒的嚴寒只有最堅韌的靈魂或被流放的人才能忍受。然而，這片土地的資源卻十分豐富，從天然氣到石油再到木材、煤炭和海產品等等，大量資源被出口到中國。俄烏戰爭爆發後，日本加入了西方對俄羅斯的制裁行列，來自長期緊密聯繫的鄰居的敵意使雙方都得不到什麼好處，算是在西伯利亞冷酷的氣候上又增添了一層政治寒冬。拋開複雜的局勢不談，這次旅程本身已足夠我大開眼界。

飛機平安降落在庫頁島，在機場迎接我們的是由俄羅斯地理學會為我們安排的當地嚮導，名叫加波年科・維塔利，他是一位退休的地理歷史教師。第一站是「薩哈林旅行記」博物館，館名同俄國著名文學家安東・契訶夫在一八九一年至一八九三年間連載的書，館址則是契訶夫當年居住於庫頁島時的舊居。契訶夫早年當過醫生，後成為知名劇作家，在他的創作生涯中，庫頁島之行絕對算得上是改變風格的轉折點。講解員安娜賽蒂莎告訴我們，這位當時已富盛名喜劇小說家在庫頁島目睹了許多令他無比震驚的事情，包括但不限於鞭刑和強迫賣淫。他在書中詳細描述了流放

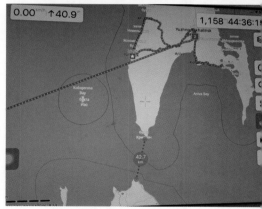

De-icing airplane / 除冰中的飛機
Sakhalin route close to Hokkaido /
靠近北海道的庫頁島航線

者所處的惡劣環境，並寫下這樣的文字：「我感覺我看到了人類墮落的極限。」之後，他的記錄和創作間接推動了西伯利亞刑罰系統的澈底改革，使其變得更加人道。博物館的展覽利用他的描寫，再現了當時被流放者可怕的生活狀態，同時還有一些早期移民在這片邊疆土地上的生活影像。

我們年輕的女講解員安娜賽蒂莎來自克羅地亞，幾個月前剛和母親搬到庫頁島。她領我們穿越展覽館的每一個角落，細心講述著早期拓荒者們勇敢無畏的探索故事，也揭示了過去那段陰暗的歷史。我們身後是一群活潑的小學生，他們也正在老師的帶領下參觀展覽，隨後在一間工作室裡坐下來，享用他們的便當。幸福的孩子們總是相似的，他們生在被幸運眷顧的地方，沒有戰爭、貧困和飢餓，無憂無慮，滿面陽光。

我提出去參觀一下當地的魚市，因為庫頁島以海產品聞名。日本對俄進行經濟制裁之前，這些海產品大多以低廉的價格越過海峽銷往北海道市場，有些只要日本價格的四分之一。一隻三公斤重的帝王蟹只要五千到六千五俄羅斯盧布，相當於五十五到七十美元。從庫頁島的南端望去，北海道僅在四十公里外，天氣晴朗時

Happy Hour snack / 歡樂時光小吃
Seafood prices / 海鮮價格

甚至可以清楚地看見它的輪廓。

魚市裡，有幾個亞裔的攤販在各自的攤位上賣著海鮮。他們是前朝鮮和日本移民的後代，如今成為了新一代的俄亞混血。他們大多已不會說自己的母語，只能講幾句簡單的日常用語。許多賣相可人的海鮮已經煮熟並放入冷凍櫃，我們果斷買了一隻色澤誘人的巨大帝王蟹帶回酒店，準備在我們的歡樂時光裡當作小吃享用。

我們的嚮導維塔利的小背包裡裝著幾本剪貼簿，他時不時會自豪地拿出來展示給我看。看起來這些是他用來教授庫頁島地理和歷史的教材。剪貼簿裡是報紙和雜誌的拼接，還有一些是從書中複製的圖片。我對他關於阿伊努人的那本相冊特別感興趣，他們是庫頁島和北海道的原住民，那些引導早期海上航運的燈塔舊照也同樣讓我著迷。還有他在鄂霍次克海的秋列尼島拍攝的照片，激起了我想在將來造訪的衝動。那裡的海岸線上擠滿了海豹和海獅，像是自然編織的毛毯。在特定季節，陡峭的懸崖邊還會擠滿黑白相間的海鴿群，整個看起來像是一局精彩的圍棋盤。

Vitaliy & his scrap book / 維塔利和他的剪貼簿
Indigenous Ainu people / 原住民阿伊努人
Faces of Sakhalin / 來自庫頁島臉龐

Cathedral of The Nativity, Orthodox church, Yuzhno Sakhalinsk /
東正教耶穌誕生大教堂，南薩哈林斯克（庫頁島）

Inside the church / 教堂內部

在薩哈林州度過的四天裡，我們還先後參觀了港口城市涅韋爾斯克的西海岸和霍爾姆斯克的東部小鎮。霍爾姆斯克的神奇之處在於，城市裡隨處可見日據時期留下的破敗建築和軍事設施，伴著裸露在地面上的石油管線和水管線。港口釣魚的人們卻彷彿完全不在意周遭的環境，不念過去，也不盼未來，只是看著眼前的大海，彷彿身在芬蘭灣。在科爾薩科夫港的南北兩端，各有一座紀念碑，標記著二戰期間日本登陸的地點。沿途，我們在一處海邊山坡上的度假村停下來享用茶點。這個度假村是二〇二三年剛開業的，客房均採用現代化設計的幾何圓頂帳篷，像是一顆顆嵌在山坡上的珍珠。這種帳篷，桿子在表面縱橫交錯，形成三角形，可以分散結構壓力，使其成為在極端天氣條件下最穩定的帳篷類型。

最後，我選擇將一座東正教教堂作為薩哈林旅程的終點。教堂內部雄偉壯麗，不同種族面孔的信徒一同佇立，默默祈禱。在這片寧靜中，我帶著心靈的平和，坐上了前往符拉迪沃斯托克的飛機。

Kholmsk harbor / 霍爾姆斯克港

踏雪披霜的西伯利亞奇行錄　第五章

WINTER EXPEDITION TO SIBERIA (Part 5)

Vladivostok, Siberia Far East – December, 2023

WINTER EXPEDITION TO SIBERIA (Part 5)

Vladivostok is home to the Russian Pacific Fleet, passed down since the former Czarist Empire rule, and later into the Soviet hands and then that of the current Russian Navy. The devastation of the entire fleet during the 1903-04 Russo-Japanese War spelled the rise of Japan which lasted through almost half of the 20th Century, until Japan's surrender at the end of WWII.

Opposite the current naval base with modern warships moored along the bay is a special exhibit of a S-56 submarine, hoisted and sat on land. The S-class sub is the most iconic and successful submarine in the Soviet Navy during WWII. Marking the entrance to the sub is another WWII icon, a Russian T-34 tank gun turret section. The displays call to mind one of the thrillers I have ever read, Tom Clancy's Hunt for Red October, later set as a movie starring Sean Connery. Whereas the T-34 became name of a latter-day Russian movie about the reassembling of a broken tank captured by the Germans during WWII, it described how the tank captured also the imagination, and ultimate escape, of a group of Russian POW from a Nazi prison camp.

Drama and political fortunes aside, Vladivostok historically owes its existence to the deep seaport that acted as a military and trading arm of the largest country in the world that extends from Europe to Far Eastern Asia, literally spanning eleven time zones. "Great" Britain may have claimed

Vladivostok by the sea / 海邊的符拉迪沃斯托克   Street scene / 海參崴街景

the sun never sets in the British Empire, counting the spread of its colonies, a long passe statement. But Russia's wide land span can probably make true claim to this notion, especially along its northernmost longitudinal region.

To move from such huge expanse of open land and cramped into the hold of a submarine is a kind of reverse metamorphosis into a cocoon. But this tiny space holds much fascination regarding time in the past, going retro into era of WWII. As somewhat of a military enthusiast regarding World War Two, I crawled through the various chambers, and looked through the periscope. Obviously, no one except the highest officers have their own bed, and sharing bunk in shifts seems to be order of the day. Imagining myself to be a new enlist, I laid for a brief moment in the bunk next to the torpedoes and their firing turrets. In real, the chamber must be super hot, despite a Siberian ice-bound winter outside.

Ironically, much to the chagrin of those who mock the Russian Navy, this S-56 was declared "dead", or sunk,

HM on T-34 Naval base in back /
T-34 坦克上的 HM，背景是海軍基地
S-56 sub / S-56 潛艇

19 times, only to resurface over and over again. Now it is pronounced "unsinkable" and is on perpetual display by the Naval Yard of Vladivostok.

Sitting above the S-56 is an Orthodox church, and below it an old building of some significance. This is home to the Russian Geographical Society (RGS), founded in 1845, with its Far East Primosrsky Krai Chapter (inclusive of Vladivostok) being one of the most important chapters. It was merged with the Society for the Study of the Amur Region. The Chairman Buyakov Aleksey Mikhailovich is our host as we sat down inside its ancient-looking conference room for a meeting.

We exchanged greetings and a brief description of each other's work. While that of the RGS goes back almost two centuries, I presented in brief CERS four decades of exploration work with pride. I admired on display some of early reports and documents in very classic fine hand writings. As a parting gift, I was given a small flag of the RGS to remember our meeting.

Apparently, the RGS takes other such organizations the like of CERS very seriously and everywhere we go, the local chapter would host us. President Putin, like many government dignitaries and royalties in the world, also gives great recognition to pioneering geographic workers throughout the ages. Putin is Chairman of the Board of Trustees of the RGS, and has presided over several anniversary functions of the Russian Geographical Society at its headquarters in St Petersburg. He had given special addresses to the esteemed scholars and geographers, citing early explorers of note within the Russian institution.

Such respect and distinction given to explorers in the West seems a far cry from the recognition we receive in the East, as our work is celebrated by a very select few within our community. At times, my work has even been mocked as being at play, without knowing all the sciences and hard work behind professional exploration. While I consider my photographic and writing skills as easy trade and eye-catching to the general public, the support I received from the National Geographic and NASA are far more indicative and of note to those with discriminating standards. Recently, University of Hong Kong's setting up of a Wong How Man Centre for Exploration in its prestigious Main Building would obviously be a big surprise for many who have considered our work a marginalized preoccupation.

It is perhaps a surprise that at this far corner of Russia the Far Eastern Federal University can rival even Moscow State University, boasting an enrollment of over 22,000 students. We made a brief visit to its campus by the sea, somewhat isolated from the city. Nearby is also the Primorsky Oceanarium, a marine museum with huge tanks of display of marine life of the North Sea.

At another corner of Vladivostok is a lighthouse that is jutted out through a rock causeway. At high tide, the ocean would obliterate the causeway. But since we arrived at low tide, we were able to walk out to the tip where the lighthouse stood. Nearby is a restaurant with a great view that we went not once, but twice, to enjoy its fine cuisine.

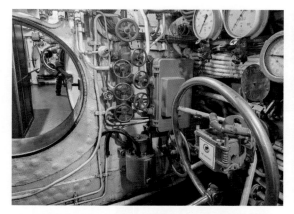

Inside S-56 / S-56 潛艇內部
Torpedo chamber / 魚雷艙
HM at periscope / HM 在潛望鏡旁

Dr Natasha our driver / 司機娜塔莎女士
Octopus Cafe by the sea / 海邊咖啡店

Tourists can arrive Vladivostok not only by flight, but also as a stopover of cruise ships. Thus along the center of the city, there are many fine restaurants and shops. We rented a van driven by a middle-aged man and wife team in rotation. The wife Natasha is a medical doctor in epidemiology. The pandemic got her working day and night over the last few years that exhausted her with burnt out, thus she now decided to quit her medical profession and joined her husband Valery in becoming a driver, plus running an auto repair shop. She found such work giving her more freedom as well as fairly good financial returns. Our van rental per day is Five Hundred USD.

Finally, our sojourn in Russia's Siberia Far East is coming to a close. I look at the map and realized that we have barely covered a tiny bit of this huge land mass. My time is short and the land is big. I must return soon to explore. Perhaps I can reach beyond the arctic belt of Siberia. Perhaps choosing not to come during a Siberia winter would be a better choice.

Lighthouse guarding Vladivostok / 守護符拉迪沃斯托克的燈塔

踏雪披霜的西伯利亞奇行錄 第五章 遠東之珠海參崴

這趟俄羅斯之行的最後一站是遠東地區的行政中心，海參崴，它也曾屬於中國。俄羅斯將其佔領後賦予了它另一個頗有深意的名字，符拉迪沃斯托克，意思大概是，擁有這座城市的國家，是整個東方的統治者。這座特別的城市是太平洋艦隊的駐地，這支艦隊自沙俄時期傳承下來，後由蘇聯接管，現在則由俄羅斯海軍掌控。一九〇三至一九〇四年的日俄戰爭中，整個艦隊遭到日本毀滅性的打擊。這一事件標誌著日本在二十世紀前半葉的崛起，直到二戰結束日本投降。

在現代軍艦停泊的海灣對面，有一個特別的展覽：一艘 S-56 潛艇被吊起，懸放在陸地上。這艘 S 級潛艇是蘇聯海軍在二戰時期最成功，也是最具標誌性的潛艇。潛艇入口處還有另一個二戰時期的標誌──一個 T-34 坦克炮塔。這些東西讓我想起曾讀過的一本驚悚小說《獵殺紅色十月》，作者是湯姆‧克蘭西，後來還被改編成了電影，由史恩‧康納萊主演。近年，俄羅斯還出了一部與 T-34 同名的電影，根據真實故事改編，講述了二戰時一群俄國戰俘利用一輛被德軍俘獲的 T-34 坦克，歷盡艱辛，最後成功逃離納粹集中營的驚險故事。

撇開影視作品和政治命運不談，歷史上，符拉迪沃斯托克這座城市的存在完全歸功於它的深水港。這個港口作為全球最大的國家從歐洲延伸到亞洲遠東的軍事和貿易樞紐，橫跨了整整十一個時區。所謂的「大」不列顛帝國曾經仗著他們的殖民地遍布全球，宣稱大英的太陽永不落下，如今看起來早已成為過去的註腳。然而，俄羅斯或許能夠真正實現這一說法，尤其是在其經度最北的地區，因其疆域實在是廣袤。

從開闊的大地，轉而擠進潛艇狹小的艙室，就像是逆向的蛻變，進入了一個繭中。這個狹小的空間充滿了對過去時光的迷戀，剛一進去就讓人感覺穿越回了二戰的年代。作為一個對二戰有著濃厚興趣的軍事愛好者，我匍匐穿過各個艙室細細觀看，還研究了一下裡面的潛望鏡。我注意到，除了最高級別的軍官外，沒有人有自己的床鋪，輪班人員是要共用鋪位的。我試著躺在緊挨著魚雷和發射塔的鋪位上，想像自己是一個新入伍的士兵，看著近在眼前的武器，我突然意識到，即使外面是西伯利亞冰封的寒冬，對當時的士兵來說，這個艙室內也一定熱得難以忍受。

諷刺的是，那些嘲笑俄羅斯海軍實力的人總是對這艘傳說被擊沉過十九次的潛艇嗤之以鼻，但卻不曾想過，為什麼每一次，它都能奇蹟般地再度浮出水面，重獲新生。如今，它被稱為「不死之艦」，永久展示在符拉迪沃斯托克的海軍基地，用它堅韌的靈魂反襯戰爭的殘酷無情。

在 S-56 潛艇上方矗立著一座東正教教堂，而在其下方則是一棟

Naval base & port / 海軍基地與港口
Russian warship / 俄羅斯軍艦

RGS Vladivostok Chapter /
俄羅斯地理學會濱海邊疆區分會
Meeting at RGS / 與俄羅斯地理學會的會談

具有重要意義的古老建築。這裡是俄羅斯地理學會的所在地，該學會成立於一八四五年，其遠東濱海邊疆區分會是最重要的分會之一，這個分會目前與研究阿穆爾地區的學會合併辦公。我們在一個古色古香的會議室內落座，分會主席布亞科夫‧阿列克謝‧米哈伊洛維奇熱情地接待了我們，並向我們簡要介紹了他們的工作。

期間，我不得不感嘆於俄羅斯地理學會可以追溯到近兩個世紀前的悠長歷史，不過我還是挺直腰板，自豪地介紹了中國探險學會四十年來的工作。我還控制不住地被那些陳列在書櫃裡的早期報告和文件吸引，那上面手寫字經典又流暢。臨走時，我收到了一面小小的俄羅斯地理學會的旗幟作為會面紀念。

顯然，俄羅斯地理學會對像中國探險學會這樣的組織非常重視，每當我們到訪一處，當地的分會都會熱情款待我們。我想這是源於一個國家對地理認知和探索工作的重視。普京總統與世界上許多政府要員和皇室成員一樣，對歷代開拓性的地理工作者給予了高度認可。目前他還是俄羅斯地理學會董事會主席，曾在聖彼得堡總部主持過多次週年慶典，並向俄羅斯的學者、地理學家和早期探險家們致辭以表敬意。

西方對探險工作的重視，和我們在東方所得到的認可相比，簡直

CERS at RGS Chapter / 中國探險學會與俄羅斯地理學會濱海邊疆區分會

是天壤之別。說實話，我們的工作只在少數人當中被認可，有時甚至被戲稱是在遊戲人生。而那些我們為了進行專業地探險而付出的辛勤勞動，甚至是探險背後嚴謹的科學邏輯，都是常常被忽略了的。雖然單單是我的攝影和寫作能力就已經足夠獲得大眾的注意和認可，但對那些「挑剔」的人來說，只有獲得美國《國家地理雜誌》和美國國家航天署(美國國家航空暨太空總署)的支持這種事，才具有價值和說服力。今天得到國際名校香港大學以我命名的探險中心進駐大學主樓，也許令很多人感覺意外吧。

說起來你可能不信，在遠離俄羅斯首都的一個偏遠角落裡，遠東聯邦大學的規模竟能和莫斯科國立大學比上一比。這座遠離城市喧囂的濱海校園裡，目前擁有超過兩萬兩千名註冊在校生。我們短暫地參觀了一下校園和附近的普里莫爾斯基海洋館，那是一座展示北海海洋生物的大型水族博物館。

在海參崴的另一端，有一座燈塔從岩石堤道中突出。漲潮時，海水會淹沒堤道，於是

Primorsky Oceannarium / 普里莫爾斯基海洋館　　　　　Display at Oceanarium / 海洋館內部展示

我們在退潮時前往，走到了燈塔所在的尖端。附近有一家風景絕佳，食物又不錯的餐館，所以我們在一天之內光顧了兩次。

遊客如果想前往海參崴，不僅可以乘飛機，還可以坐那些會停靠在市區內的郵輪。因此，市中心有許多高級餐廳和商店。我們租了一輛由一對中年夫妻輪流駕駛的麵包車。妻子娜塔莎原是一位流行病學醫生。過去幾年的疫情期間，她日夜工作，身心俱疲，因此決定退出醫療行業，與丈夫瓦列里一起經營一家汽修店，時不時出車當司機。她發現這樣的工作不僅給了她更多的自由，還有相當不錯的報酬，用於參考，我們每天的租車費是五百美元。

至此，我們在俄羅斯西伯利亞遠東地區的旅程已然接近尾聲。看著地圖，才驚覺我們只是觸及了這片廣袤土地的小小一角。時間短暫，而大地遼闊，我必須儘快再回來探索。下次我計畫越過西伯利亞的北極圈，去探索更加偏遠神祕的地區。不過或許避開西伯利亞的冬季來訪，會是一個更明智的決定。

Far Eastern Federal Univ / 遠東聯邦大學

Mural at Vladivostok / 街頭壁畫

新
三
國
志

THREE KINGDOMS

Dalian – December, 2023

Dalian – December, 2023

THREE KINGDOMS
Where China, Russia & North Korea meet, and beyond

Competition or complementation; it is a choice for nations which are neighbors to each other. I have often said, friends from afar can come and go. But your neighbors, especially in the form of neighboring countries, will always stay, whether you like them or not. In that, you have a choice, to work toward being a friend or a foe. Given the wrong choice, you can see perpetual hostility, like what we are witnessing around many other parts of the world.

Forming alliances to leverage against stronger neighbors is a stop-gap measure. Building trust and friendship is more long-lasting. Faraway nations, with self-interests packaged as high-sounding motives, syndicating by coercion or arm-twisting as countermeasure, is evidence that they cannot provide the balance on their own. It is usually done at a time when the tipping point of an adversary, real or imagined, has passed or is nearing. If they alone can handle an issue, there will be no need to form alliances, be they for defense or offence.

Recently, we have seen such models repeated around the world. If not harnessed well, these maneuvers can lead to war. I recalled a poem I wrote when I attended the University of Wisconsin in Journalism in 1972. The point I made may still be valid fifty years later. "A battle won or a battle lost, there is little difference in the cost, winner or loser they die all the same, but for commanders it is just a game."

Can we turn a conflict of interest into a complementary interest? Optimists would say yes, pessimists otherwise. History may play a role in it. History, however, is often brutal rather than kind.

With such questions in my mind, I left Russia's Siberia Far East from Vladivostok and traveled to Hun Chun, a frontier city sandwiched between Russia and North Korea. I went on afterwards to visit Dandong, Dalian and Lushun, three important cities of Liaoning Province extending into the peninsula. Change of fortune, or misfortune, in contemporary history has seen two of these cities change ownership several times.

First, Hun Chun — that piece of meat between two pieces of bread, especially now that China has become the frontrunner in economic terms among the three countries of Russia, North Korea and China. It resonates somewhat with the turbulent history of the Three Kingdoms era in Chinese history almost two thousand years ago.

Hun Chun is sandwiched between two rather formidable countries, Russia and North Korea. On the Russian side is Zhang Gu Feng (張鼓峰), a

Japan casualties on hospital ship 1905 /
1905 年醫務船上的日本傷員
Old books & albums of the past / 過去的舊書和相本

famous battleground between Japan and the former Soviet Union which lasted for eleven days in 1938 right before WWII. By some accounts, it is said to have given inspiration to the Russian song Katyusha, composed by Matvey Blanter with lyrics written by the soviet poet Mikhail Isakovsky. The song is now world-famous, played and sung as a military marching song about a Russian lover saying goodbye to a soldier leaving for the front. (If you cannot remember the tune, search on YouTube.)

Katyusha is also a nickname for the much-feared Russian missile launcher of WWII. So it was here where Katyusha was home that we drove right into the pincer of this long strip of land, just a short distance from the delta mouth of the Tumen River (圖們江). Verging on the ocean but cannot quite reach it, it forks and flows into the coastlines of Russia and North Korea. This is China's much sought-after access to the sea, yet so far. It was said that some discussion has been

Bridge connecting Russia with N. Korea /
連接俄羅斯與北韓的鐵路橋

Border tablet between Russia & China /
俄羅斯與中國之間的土字牌界碑

underway with Russia to allow ocean access in the future, thus making Jilin Province being able to exit and enter from the ocean with a much-needed maritime opening.

At the tip of China's corridor land, we climbed some stairs surrounded by barbed wire to higher ground, looking beyond the fence, at a steel bridge for trains a couple of kilometers away which connects Russia to North Korea. The open sea is beyond and within sight, so near yet so far away and unreachable. Right at the border is a stone tablet, human height, bearing the three characters in Chinese, "Tu Zi Pai" (土字牌), meaning "Cross Word Tablet". It is the first and starting border marking along the long inland border between Russia and China.

Today the tablet is enclosed in a glass case and designated a National Historical Monument five years ago. It comes to signify how a mandarin official of the Qing Dynasty chaffered hard in 1886 to regain just a little area covering some twenty kilometers after a huge loss of territories of some 440,000 square kilometers to Czarist Russia in the war of 1860, which is now a humongous part of the Russian Far East. Such humiliating history of a weakening Qing Dynastic Empire is a reminder for current China to build its nation to be strong, not just economically but also militarily in order to defend its borders.

Leaving Hun Chun, we traveled along Yalu River (鴨綠江) which defines the border between China and North Korea, arriving at the frontier city of Dandong, thus leaving Jilin Province into Liaoning Province. Here was the site of major confrontation during the Korean War when the US and its "Allied" Forces pushed north all the way past the 38th Parallel to the bank of the Yalu, precipitating China's response to enter the War with its volunteer army, well-seasoned through the protracted war against the Japanese followed by Civil War against Chiang Kai-shek's nationalist army. It successfully pushed back US forces to far south beyond the 38th Parallel before a truce *was called that ended in a stalemate, with the two Koreas still divided to this day at the so-called "demilitarized" zone, benefiting the wildlife to roam freely with little danger of being shot at.*

We stayed at a hotel within walking distance of the famous, or infamous, Broken Bridge over the Yalu. This revolving swing bridge of steel was first built by the Japanese in 1911 at the close of the Qing Dynasty, connecting by rail Dandong on China's side with the Korean city of Sinuiju. At that time, Korea was under Japanese rule and much of Manchuria was also under the control and influence of Japan. The bridge was bombed by US warplanes in 1951 and remained only half intact, reaching the middle of the Yalu River.

Visitors would walk the bridge lined with description boards to revisit the history of that era. On both sides of the Yalu, China and North Korea, there are some high-rise modern buildings. At night the China side is full of colorful neon lights. But on the east side of the river, it is almost pitch dark, making one wonder whether there are actual residents in those buildings. In the morning, however, the sun would rise from behind those modern façades of buildings.

At our next stop Dalian, I insisted on finding a homestay hotel by the fishing port in order to have a look at boats coming back with their catch. It is part of my current interest, developed over the last couple of years, to visit fishing ports along China's coast to understand more about the fishing industry. Heavy snow fell in the evening and the boats were covered with a layer of white, with the causeway ending at a nicely lit-up lighthouse. The blue and yellow tone made it almost dreamingly European, as if from an Art Deco retro age.

From Dalian, it is only an hour's drive to the strategic port city of Lushun, also known in the West as Port Arthur. Here my interest goes back in history, as I have been collecting books and old maps of this very important naval harbor that had been the contention of imperial powers for over a century, first between the Manchu Qing court and Japan in 1894, and later between Russia and Japan during the Russo-Japanese War of 1904. These battles happened despite that both Dalian and Lushun were within the precinct of China at the tip of the Liaoning Peninsular.

Steam boat on Songhua River / 松花江上汽船

Japanese drawing of sea battle / 日軍海戰圖
Japanese photo of Russia fleet sunk /
日本拍攝的俄羅斯艦隊被擊沉的照片

The most decisive battle that sealed the fate of Lushun was in 1904 when the entire Russian Far East fleet was destroyed by the navy of Admiral Togo. A year later, even the Baltic fleet was decimated when it was dispatched to the East. Several books in my collection, published in Japan right at the closing of that war, depicted in drawings and photographs about the heroic Japanese army while mocking the defeat of the Russian Imperial Navy. A map published in 1935 that I recently obtained in Tokyo can also shed light on the very strategic location of this coastal port city.

Several photo albums about Lushun I acquired further show how much infrastructure and massive buildings were constructed by the Japanese following their winning of the war over Czarist Russia. We visited one such site, the history museum at Lushun. Not only is the building in Japanese style of the early 20th century, but much of the interior displays and even the large and elaborate cases also come to show that the Japanese must have considered this war spoils their permanent possession, bringing even some of their valued collection from Japan to be placed inside this museum.

My last stop of this sojourn which started in Siberia during the depth of winter finally ended with Lushun, or Port Arthur. Today peace has finally returned to this beautiful natural harbor. It is perhaps a well-earned peace. I stood at the port side inside the bay, contemplating and watching *a constant flow of fishing boats returning to port. I observed fresh catch being passed up the embankment, with anxious buyers waiting with their cars or trucks. I know it is time for me and my team to also hit the local restaurant to quench our hunger pang. Ordering a meal of seafood at reasonable and discounted prices.*

These very fine products of the ocean would naturally escalate in price, as they are transported further and further inland to feed an insatiable market of a massive population now affluent enough to enjoy seafood even in the deepest corner of China. Such affluence, however, should not be taken for granted. As peace and prosperity are fought over with blood and tears of our forefathers.

As closing on an article much about war and peace, I must merit the Asian people for being so forgiving to the Japanese, and the Japanese in turn being so forgiving too to the two atomic bombs dropped on two civilian cities, and be gracious enough to form new alliances with former adversaries.

Japanese battle front portrayal / 日俄戰場
Drawing of Russian surrender / 俄國投降圖
Admiral Togo receiving surrender on ship / 東鄉將軍在船上接受投降

新三國志

在中俄朝交界聆聽遠方的迴響

惡性競爭還是相輔相成，是處理鄰國關係時必須面對的關鍵抉擇。我經常說，你可以不在乎遠方朋友的種種，因為他們總是來來去去，但你的「鄰居」，無論你是否喜歡，他們都會一直在那裡。在和「鄰居」的相處中，你通常沒有模棱兩可的選擇，要麼努力成為朋友，要麼，就成為敵人。如果選擇錯誤，你將會被永無止境的敵意包圍，紛擾纏身，就像當今世界許多地方正在發生的情況一樣。

用所謂的結盟來對抗強大的鄰居只是權宜之計，建立信任和友誼才是長久之道。一些孤懸海外的國家，總是以高尚的名義包裝自己，掩蓋其謀取私利的企圖。不斷脅迫他國組建小團體的行為也恰恰暴露了一個現實問題，就是他們無法獨自維持自己想要的平衡，無論獲取平衡的手段是主動進攻還是被動防守。國家和國家之間總是忌憚著彼此的實力，一旦一方主觀性地認為對面已經構成威脅，越過紅線，那麼拉幫結派，各種層面的制裁就會隨之而來，一不小心，就會演變成武力衝突。

當今世界，上述境況屢見不鮮。這使我想起一九七二年我在威斯康辛學新聞時寫的一首詩。我認為即使已經過了五十年，這個觀點依然不過時。「勝負代價幾無差，輸贏同歸盡，塵土無話。惟有將軍心，視之如棋局，笑中藏刀花。」

所以，我們能否將利益衝突化為互惠互利呢？或許只有樂觀者會
說能，悲觀者則不以為然。歷史在我眼中多數時候是殘酷而非仁
慈的，那麼它在如今的國際政治中又能起到怎樣的作用呢？

懷著這些疑問，我離開了俄羅斯的遠東地區，從海參崴出發，前
往夾在俄羅斯和北韓之間的邊境城市——吉林琿春。隨後，我又
拜訪了遼寧省的三個重要城市：丹東、大連和旅順。近代歷史的
變遷，曾使其中兩座城市多次易主。

我們首先來到了琿春——這個夾在兩個大國之間的小地方。它看
起來就像是夾在兩塊麵包當中的肉，特別是在中國已經成為鄰國
間經濟領跑者的今天。這不禁讓人聯想到兩千年前，那個動盪的
三國時代。

在琿春市靠近圖們江入海口，中俄的邊境線上，有一個小山包，
名叫張鼓峰，這裡是一九三八年二戰前夕，日本與蘇聯激戰了
十一天的戰場。據說這場戰役是俄羅斯著名傳統民謠＜喀秋莎＞
的靈感來源。這首由馬特維‧布蘭特作曲，米哈伊爾‧伊薩科夫
斯基填詞的歌曲，如今已成為世界聞名的軍事進行曲，講述了一
位俄羅斯女孩盼望守衛邊疆的愛人早日歸來的故事。＜喀秋莎＞
同時也是二戰中令人聞風喪膽的俄羅斯火箭炮的綽號。如果說到
這你還想不起那優美的旋律，可以去 *YouTube* 上搜一搜。

Japanese map circa 1935 showing occupied
Sakhalin, Korea & Lushun /
1935 年左右的日本地圖，包含當時被佔領的
薩哈林島、北韓和旅順

Barbed-wire border / 用鐵絲網攔起的國界
Swing bridge circa. 1931 /
1931 年日本建設的可旋轉鴨綠江鐵橋

我們駕車沿著張鼓峰所在的狹長地帶駛去，道路旁的圖們江水奔騰不息。這條河流在馬上投入海洋的懷抱時兵分兩路，分別流入俄羅斯和北韓的海岸。張鼓峰戰役後，日本和蘇聯封鎖了中國夢寐以求的圖們江出海口，如今，這個海上通道已沉寂了近百年。不過據說，今年中俄雙方正在積極討論中國船隻經由圖們江下游出海的相關事宜，如果圖們江出海口得以暢通，那麼不僅是吉林省和整個東北地區，連同俄羅斯和北韓也能從中受益。

在狹長國界線的盡頭，我們沿著被鐵絲網包圍的階梯攀登到了一方高處。透過圍欄遠望，可以看到幾公里外的一座鐵路大橋，連接著俄羅斯和北韓。開闊的海洋就在眼前，近在咫尺卻遙不可及。邊界上矗立著一塊跟人差不多高的石碑，上刻「土字牌」三個大字，這是中俄漫長內陸邊界線的第一塊界碑。

這塊界碑如今被安置在玻璃罩內，並於五年前被指定為全國重點文物保護單位。它不僅僅是一塊界碑，更是中華民族愛國精神的象徵。一八八六年，在中國失去約四十四萬平方公里土地二十六年後，清朝官員吳大澂終於尋得機會，透過不屈不撓的，長達三個月的艱苦談判，將「土字牌」向沙草峰挪前約 20 里，收回了今天琿春市敬信鎮的全境。這段屈辱的歷史告訴現代中國，唯有軍事與經濟並重，才能真正捍衛國土，保證國家安全。

Barbed broken bridge today / 如今的鴨綠江斷橋

Sunrise over N. Korea / 北韓的日出
Route map of where three countries met /
三國交界路線圖

離開琿春，從吉林省進入遼寧省，我們沿著鴨綠江前行，抵達了另一座邊境城市丹東。鴨綠江劃定了中國與北韓的邊界，而丹東曾是朝鮮戰爭的主要戰場。一九五〇年，美國及其「聯合國軍」一路北推，越過三八線直逼鴨綠江邊，迫使中國派出經歷過抗日戰爭和內戰的「中國人民志願軍」應戰。三年苦戰後，志願軍最終成功地將美軍推回三八線以南，達成停戰協議，建立「朝韓非軍事區」作為緩衝地帶。如今這片非軍事區成了野生動物的天堂，無需擔心遭到射擊，牠們活得自由自在，彷彿朝鮮半島的緊張局勢從不存在。

我們入住了一家距離著名的鴨綠江斷橋僅步行可達的江邊酒店。這座旋轉鋼橋由日本人在清末一九一一年建造，鐵路連接中國的丹東市和朝鮮的新義州。當時，朝鮮處於日本統治之下，大部分滿洲也在日本的控制和影響之中。這座橋在一九五一年被美國戰機轟炸後只剩下半截，延伸到鴨綠江的中間。

今天的鴨綠江斷橋已成為一個景區，遊客可以步行在橋上，閱讀沿途描述歷史的展板。鴨綠江兩岸，中國和北韓都有一些現代高層建築。夜晚，中國這一側燈火輝煌，霓虹色彩斑斕。而江的東側卻幾乎漆黑一片，讓人不禁懷疑那些樓裡是否真的有人居住。不過第二天清晨，當朝陽從名為「太陽樓」的圓形建築後緩緩升起，金色的光芒灑在江面上，鴨綠江在晨曦中閃閃發光時，我才感到江東的景色也別有一番風味。

我們的下一站是大連。我堅持要在漁港旁找一家民宿來住，以便觀察漁船歸港的景象。這是我近兩年來的一個興趣所在，走訪中國沿海的漁港，了解中國漁業的現狀。傍晚時分，大雪紛飛，漁船覆蓋上一層潔白的雪衣。堤道的盡頭是一座燈火通明的燈塔，藍色和黃色的光影交織，彷彿讓人回到二十世紀的歐洲，那個裝飾派藝術風格蓬勃發展的夢幻年代。

從大連出發，只需一小時車程便可抵達古今戰略要地，也是我頗感興趣的城市旅順，西方稱之為亞瑟港。我一直在收集有關這個重要海軍港口的書籍和古地圖。這個港口曾經是帝國力量角逐的焦點，先是一八九四年清朝與日本在此交戰，後有一九〇四年日俄戰爭，兩軍在此爭奪主權。儘管這裡是遼東半島尖端的中國領土，但不斷蔓延的炮火讓大連和旅順數次化身國際爭端的舞台。

一九〇四年，決定旅順命運的關鍵戰役爆發，日本海軍軍官東鄉平八郎的艦隊全殲了俄國遠東艦隊。一年後，俄國派遣的波羅地海艦隊也在東方被徹底摧毀。我收藏的幾本舊書，是在戰爭結束時期於日本出版的，書中的照片詳細描繪了日軍的英勇事跡，同時還不忘嘲諷俄羅斯帝國海軍的潰敗。我最近在東京獲得的一張一九三五年出版的地圖，也清晰展示了這座沿海港口城市的重要

Japanese war map of Lushun 1931 /
1931 年抗日戰爭時期日本繪製的旅順市規劃地圖
Japanese & Russian army generals meeting /
日本和俄羅斯將軍會面

戰略位置。

我還收集到幾個日本出版的旅順舊時寫真帖。它們進一步展示了日本在戰勝沙俄後，在旅順建設的大量基礎設施和功能性建築。我們參觀了其中一處，「旅順歷史博物館」。這座博物館建於二十世紀初期，從外觀到內部裝修，完完全全是日式風格。從那些價值不菲的展品和展櫃也不難看出，日本人當年是將這些戰利品視為永久財產的，甚至他們還將一些珍貴的收藏品從日本帶到這裡來展出。

我的冬季旅程從西伯利亞的嚴寒中開始，也至此，在旅順歷史的低語中畫上了句號。如今，這個美麗的天然港口終於迎來了它來之不易的，應得的和平。我站在港口邊，看著一艘艘漁船在夕陽的餘暉中緩緩駛回港灣，新鮮的漁獲被迅速傳上堤岸，買家們早已在此等候多時，忙忙碌碌，準備接收豐盛的成果。此情此景，讓我想起，是時候和我的團隊一起去當地餐館享用一頓豐盛的海鮮大餐了。

這些來自大海的珍饈，從小漁港一路運往內地各處，價格自然會逐步攀升。如今，即便是在中國的最偏遠角落，人們也能享用到海鮮，這無疑是這個國家繁榮昌盛的具象體現。然而，我不禁想到，這樣的富足並非理所當然。今日的安寧與繁榮，是先輩們以鮮血和淚水換來的，歷史的聲音揮之不去，提醒我們珍惜當下。

在這篇探討戰爭與和平文章的結尾，我不得不感慨於亞洲人民的寬容。他們能夠原諒日本的侵略，而日本也能夠原諒那兩顆投在無辜平民城市上的原子彈，並與昔日的敵人握手言和，建立新的同盟。

Dalian under Japanese occupation 1931 /1931 年的日據大連
Dalian Japanese Rail headquarters 1931 / 1931 年設立在大連的南滿鐵路總局

國家圖書館出版品預行編目 (CIP) 資料

齊物逍遙 . 2024. I I= Enlightened sojourn/ 黃效文著 . -- 初版 .
-- 新北市 : 依揚想亮人文事業有限公司 , 2024.11
面 ; 公分
中英對照
ISBN 978-626-96174-7-0(精裝)
1.CST: 遊記 2.CST: 世界地理
719   113015219

齊物逍遙 2024 II

作者・黃效文｜攝影・黃效文｜發行人・劉鋆｜美術編輯・Rene、鍾京燕｜責任編輯・廖又蓉｜翻譯・呂怡達｜法律顧問・達文西個資暨高科技法律事務所｜出版社・依揚想亮人文事業有限公司｜經銷商・聯合發行股份有限公司｜地址・新北市新店區寶橋路 235 巷 6 弄 6 號 2 樓｜電話・02 2917 8022｜印刷・禹利電子分色有限公司｜初版一刷・2024 年 11 月（精裝）｜定價 1500 元｜ISBN・978-626-96174-7-0｜版權所有 翻印必究｜Print in Taiwan